STELLA BLACKWELL

Summertime Vegan

VIBRANT GLUTEN-FREE SEASONAL DELIGHTS

Summertime Vegan

Welcome to a vibrant world of flavors, where deliciousness meets wholesome goodness! As the sun shines brighter, and the days grow longer, it's time to embrace the joy of summer with a collection of mouthwatering recipes that cater to your gluten-free and vegan lifestyle. In this book, you'll discover a treasure trove of delightful breakfasts, delectable desserts, refreshing smoothies, and savory dishes, all thoughtfully crafted to celebrate the beauty of the season.

Summertime Vegan: Vibrant Gluten-Free Seasonal Delights is a culinary journey that invites you to savor the abundance of nature's bounty. Whether you're a seasoned plant-based enthusiast or just beginning your gluten-free adventure, this cookbook is filled with an array of dishes that will leave you craving more. Every recipe is meticulously designed to deliver a burst of flavors, a touch of nourishment, and the satisfaction of knowing you're making conscious choices for yourself and the planet.

As you flip through these pages, you will find a quick introduction about the Vegan and Gluten-Free diet. Afterwards, you will experience the magic of sun-kissed mornings filled with the lusciousness of Acai Bowls and the refreshing bliss of Tropical Smoothie Bowls. Relish the creamy indulgence of Chia Seed Pudding Parfait, the fragrant Coconut Mango Rice Pudding, and the heartwarming goodness of Overnight Oats. The breakfast and sweet treats collection will make you eager to rise and shine every day, eager to embrace the possibilities summer has to offer.

Quench your thirst with a variety of invigorating smoothies and drinks that capture the essence of the season. Be it the energizing Green Protein Smoothie or the exotic Mango Lassi, the invigorating Iced Coffee Smoothie, or the soothing Iced Matcha Latte—each sip will take you on a tantalizing journey of taste and wellness. And to keep you refreshed throughout the day, explore an assortment of homemade popsicles, like the zesty Lemon-Raspberry and the tropical Piña Colada Popsicles, that will transport you to the carefree days of summers past.

The lunch and dinner selections embrace the vibrant colors and diverse flavors of seasonal produce. Dive into the Mediterranean allure of Greek Souvlaki with Tzatziki, delight in the fusion of flavors in Vegan Sushi Rolls, and indulge in the comforting goodness of Lentil Shepherd's Pie. From light and refreshing salads to hearty main courses, each dish is a celebration of fresh ingredients and creative combinations.

Join this culinary escapade and discover how easy it is to create nourishing, wholesome, and scrumptious dishes that resonate with the essence of summer. These recipes are more than just food; they are an expression of love for the environment, compassion for all living beings, and a desire to make a positive impact with every bite.

Welcome to Summertime Vegan: Vibrant Gluten-Free Seasonal Delights—where delicious meets conscious, and every bite is a celebration of summer!

Why Vegan?

In recent times, there has been a notable surge in the embrace of plant-based diets, driven by a growing consciousness about personal health and environmental sustainability. Among these conscientious dietary choices, the combination of a plant-based, vegan, and gluten-free lifestyle has captured the hearts of many seeking a wholesome approach to nourishment. But a question often arises: Can one truly flourish while excluding all animal products and gluten? In this article, we will delve deep into the heart of this innovative dietary journey, discovering how it can be a profoundly nourishing and fulfilling path to follow.

The Heart of the Vegan Lifestyle

At the core of a plant-based, vegan diet lies the essence of eschewing all animal-derived foods, including meat, dairy, eggs, and even honey. Instead, it revolves around embracing nature's abundant offerings of fruits, vegetables, legumes, nuts, seeds, and wholesome grains. By wholeheartedly embracing this dietary choice, individuals can unlock a treasure trove of health benefits, such as nurturing a healthier heart, lowering cholesterol levels, and improving weight management.

However, this journey extends far beyond personal wellness. The decision to adopt a vegan lifestyle carries profound implications for the well-being of our planet. Animal agriculture significantly contributes to environmental issues, including greenhouse gas emissions, deforestation, and water pollution. By embracing plant-based foods, we become purposeful custodians of a more sustainable future, tenderly caring for our Earth's precious resources.

Navigating the Gluten-Free Adventure

For those with celiac disease or gluten sensitivity, gluten poses a genuine challenge. Adopting a gluten-free lifestyle becomes vital to avoid digestive discomfort and long-term health complications. However, combining this with a vegan approach calls for thoughtful consideration.

Thankfully, there is a rich variety of naturally gluten-free plant-based foods waiting to be explored. From nourishing rice and quinoa to comforting potatoes, lentils, and chickpeas, nature provides us with a plethora of delectable options. Moreover, numerous companies offer gluten-free alternatives to wheat-based products, including bread, pasta, and flour.

Navigating being Gluten-Free

For those with celiac disease or gluten sensitivity, gluten poses a genuine challenge. Adopting a gluten-free lifestyle becomes vital to avoid digestive discomfort and long-term health complications. However, combining this with a vegan approach calls for thoughtful consideration.

Thankfully, there is a rich variety of naturally gluten-free plant-based foods waiting to be explored. From nourishing rice and quinoa to comforting potatoes, lentils, and chickpeas, nature provides us with a plethora of delectable options. Moreover, numerous companies offer gluten-free alternatives to wheat-based products, including bread, pasta, and flour.

Choose Whole Foods

When venturing into the world of gluten-free products offered by companies, it is essential to make mindful choices. While these alternatives can be convenient and satisfying, some may contain unwanted ingredients like excessive additives, fillers, or high levels of sugar and salt to compensate for taste and texture. Reading labels diligently and opting for products with minimal and recognizable ingredients is crucial to maintaining a healthful gluten-free vegan diet.

However, this journey extends far beyond personal wellness. The decision to adopt a vegan lifestyle carries profound implications for the well-being of our planet. Animal agriculture significantly contributes to environmental issues, including greenhouse gas emissions, deforestation, and water pollution. By embracing plant-based foods, we become purposeful custodians of a more sustainable future, tenderly caring for our Earth's precious resources.

Navigating the Gluten-Free Adventure

For those with celiac disease or gluten sensitivity, gluten poses a genuine challenge. Adopting a gluten-free lifestyle becomes vital to avoid digestive discomfort and long-term health complications. However, combining this with a vegan approach calls for thoughtful consideration.

Thankfully, there is a rich variety of naturally gluten-free plant-based foods waiting to be explored. From nourishing rice and quinoa to comforting potatoes, lentils, and chickpeas, nature provides us with a plethora of delectable options. Moreover, numerous companies offer gluten-free alternatives to wheat-based products, including bread, pasta, and flour.

Essential Micronutrients

Essential Micronutrients in a Plant-Based, Vegan, Gluten-Free Diet

To thrive on this journey, it's essential to maintain a well-balanced diet that fulfills our body's nutritional needs. Certain micronutrients warrant special attention:

1. **Vitamin B12:** As a nutrient primarily found in animal products, vitamin B12 plays a crucial role in nerve function and red blood cell production. Vegans may opt for fortified foods or supplements to meet their B12 requirements.
2. **Iron**: Our plant-based friends such as lentils, tofu, quinoa, and pumpkin seeds bless us with iron. Pairing these foods with vitamin C-rich options, like citrus fruits or bell peppers, enhances iron absorption.
3. **Calcium**: Building strong bones and teeth is possible through fortified plant-based milk, tofu, almonds, and leafy greens like kale and broccoli.
4. **Omega-3 Fatty Acids:** To nourish our brains and reduce inflammation, we can rely on flaxseeds, chia seeds, hemp seeds, and walnuts, as they offer essential omega-3 fatty acids.

5. **Vitamin D**: A delightful rendezvous with sunlight enables our bodies to produce vitamin D. We can also find this essential nutrient in fortified plant-based milk and certain mushrooms.

Conclusion

Embarking on a plant-based, vegan, and gluten-free adventure is indeed a rewarding journey—one that nurtures our bodies and the planet we call home. By savoring a diverse array of plant foods, we can thrive while reducing our environmental impact. However, like all remarkable endeavors, this one requires mindful planning to ensure we meet our essential micronutrient and macronutrient needs.

Before fully embracing this path, it's essential to seek guidance from healthcare professionals or registered dietitians, who can help tailor the diet to our individual needs, optimizing our health and well-being. With a harmonious approach, we can flourish on this compassionate and sustainable expedition, becoming guardians of our own health and our precious planet's well-being.

Seasonal Availability

Nourishing Our Planet and Bodies

The Wholesome Appeal of Seasonal Eating and Shopping

In our fast-paced world, it's easy to overlook the beauty of syncing our diets with the changing seasons. Yet, in embracing the age-old practice of seasonal eating and shopping, we discover a pathway to not only nurture our bodies but also protect our planet. This mindful approach to food selection brings forth an array of health benefits while leaving a lighter ecological footprint. Join us on this delectable journey as we explore the harmonious union of nature's bounty and our well-being.

Reduced Environmental Impact

By delighting in seasonal produce, we support local farmers and make strides in reducing the need for extensive transportation and refrigeration. Such thoughtful choices pave the way for lowered greenhouse gas emissions and energy consumption, ultimately fostering a healthier planet for all.

Preserving Biodiversity

In cherishing the fruits and vegetables that flourish during specific seasons, we celebrate the diversity of nature's offerings.

This conscious embrace of variety not only enriches our nutritional intake but also plays a crucial role in preserving biodiversity and safeguarding our ecosystems.

Improved Nutritional Value

The wisdom of seasonal eating bestows upon us produce that is naturally ripened and brimming with nutritional goodness. These locally harvested treasures boast higher levels of essential vitamins, minerals, and life-enriching phytonutrients, nurturing our well-being from within.

Supporting Local Economies

As we relish the bounty of each season, we also extend our hand in support to local farmers and artisans. This compassionate act directly contributes to the thriving of our communities, fostering sustainable local economies. Together, we build a resilient and interconnected food system that echoes with harmony.

Encouraging Sustainability

In our quest for seasonal treasures, we rediscover traditional cooking techniques and the art of food preservation. The appreciation for surplus seasonal produce leads us to embrace practices like canning and fermenting, minimizing waste and embracing a more sustainable lifestyle.

With each passing season, we find ourselves drawn closer to the rhythmic dance of nature's offerings. The path of seasonal eating and shopping beckons us to tread gently upon the earth while cherishing the essence of nourishing, flavorful delights. Let us savor the wholesome appeal of this mindful approach, nurturing both our planet and our bodies, hand in hand.

A Journey Back to Seasonal Eating

In our fast-paced world, we find ourselves drifting away from the age-old practice of seasonal eating, once cherished by our ancestors. Our plates have become adorned with the allure of year-round convenience, distancing us from the natural rhythms of the earth's bounty. As we pause to reflect on this departure, we come to realize that rediscovering seasonal eating is the path to nurturing our well-being and forging a deeper connection with the environment we call home.

The Winds of Globalization

The marvels of modern transportation and food preservation have opened doors to the global market, granting us access to an array of exotic foods throughout the year. Yet, in our quest for variety, we may overlook the environmental cost of long-distance transportation, contributing to increased carbon emissions.

A Balance between Nature and Storage

Our love for out-of-season produce has given rise to extensive storage and processing practices. Sadly, fruits and vegetables are often picked prematurely, robbing them of their natural goodness. Cold storage and chemical treatments preserve appearances but may compromise the taste and nutrient richness we desire.

The Dance of Mass Production

The wheels of progress have turned agriculture into an industry of scale. Large-scale mono-cropping and the use of synthetic inputs ensure a steady supply of certain crops, but at the expense of disregarding their natural seasonal cycles.

The Heart of Consumer Expectations

For convenience, we have come to expect a year-round abundance of produce. Our desires have shaped the global food supply chain, pushing the boundaries of what nature's seasons provide.

Seasonal Eating Nurtures our Soil

The Dance of Mass Production

The wheels of progress have turned agriculture into an industry of scale. Large-scale mono-cropping and the use of synthetic inputs ensure a steady supply of certain crops, but at the expense of disregarding their natural seasonal cycles.

The Heart of Consumer Expectations

For convenience, we have come to expect a year-round abundance of produce. Our desires have shaped the global food supply chain, pushing the boundaries of what nature's seasons provide.

How Seasonal Eating Nurtures Soil Health and Nutrient Cycles

As we embrace the beauty of seasonal eating and reconnect with the earth's bountiful offerings, it is essential to explore the profound impact this practice has on the very foundation of our nourishment— the soil. Seasonal eating, with its natural ebb and flow of produce, plays a vital role in nurturing soil health and maintaining nutrient cycles. This harmonious relationship between the food we eat and the soil beneath our feet is a testament to the sustainable dance of nature.

Soil Regeneration and Fertility

Seasonal crops, carefully chosen to flourish during specific times of the year, contribute to soil regeneration. Different crops have unique nutrient requirements, and by rotating them seasonally, we enhance soil fertility. Crop rotation helps prevent nutrient depletion and soil erosion, preserving the health of the land for future generations.

Reduced Need for Chemical Inputs

Adhering to seasonal eating principles reduces our demand for out-of-season produce, which often necessitates extensive chemical inputs to support growth. By consuming locally and seasonally, we lessen the reliance on synthetic fertilizers and pesticides, promoting a more environmentally friendly and sustainable agriculture.

Minimizing Soil Erosion

The cultivation of seasonally appropriate crops provides natural ground cover during different times of the year. This minimizes soil exposure to the elements and helps prevent erosion caused by wind and rain. Healthy soil structure, nurtured by seasonal choices, anchors and protects valuable topsoil from depletion.

Returning Nutrients to the Soil

As we consume fresh, seasonal produce, the nutrients within those foods find their way back to the soil through organic waste and composting. This cyclical process enriches the soil with vital nutrients, perpetuating the ecosystem's balance and nourishing future crops.

As we delve into the interconnected dance of seasonal eating, we uncover the intrinsic relationship between our food and the soil it is grown in. This mindful practice goes beyond the bounds of our plates; it becomes an act of stewardship and gratitude towards the earth that sustains us. By embracing seasonal eating, we honor the nurturing power of the soil, preserving its fertility and ensuring the continued nourishment of our bodies and the generations to come.

While embracing seasonal eating offers numerous benefits, it's important to acknowledge that consuming some non-seasonal foods in moderation can still be a part of a balanced diet. The availability of certain foods year-round allows for dietary diversity and culinary exploration. Additionally, some non-seasonal foods, like certain fruits and vegetables, are often preserved through freezing or canning, retaining some of their nutritional value. However, it is crucial to be mindful of the environmental impact and consider choosing locally sourced or sustainably produced options when indulging in non-seasonal treats. As long as we strike a balance between seasonal and non-seasonal choices, we can savor the best of both worlds.

June

Strawberries	Asparagus	Basil	Peas
Cherries	Broccoli	Chives	Radishes
Blueberries	Carrots	Cilantro	Cucumber
Apricots	Lettuce	Dill	Rhubarb
Pineapple	Spinach	Oregano	Purslane
Mangoes	Swiss Chard	Rosemary	Elderberries
Papayas	Artichokes	Lavender	Mulberries
Melon	Arugula	Lemon Balm	Fava Beans
Kiwi	Fennel	Mint	Bok Choy
Avocados	Peppers (Bell)	Tarragon	Kohlrabi
Guavas	Snap Peas	Sage	Currants
Limes	Beets	Chamomile	Cherimoya

July

Raspberries	Bell Peppers	Parsley	Green Beans
Blackberries	Corn	Thyme	Fennel
Peaches	Cucumbers	Sage	Eggplant
Nectarines	Tomatoes	Rosemary	Zucchini
Plums	Eggplant	Cilantro	Melons
Apricots	Summer Squash	Oregano	Napa Cabbage
Watermelon	Okra	Mint	Scallions
Cantaloupe	Green Onions	Dill	Boysenberries
Kiwi	Lima Beans	Chervil	Loganberries
Figs	Wax Beans	Lovage	Mulberries
Blueberries	Beets	Lemongrass	Chard
Currants	Radishes	Tarragon	Pluots

August

Blueberries	Green Beans	Mint	Watermelon
Plums	Tomatoes	Cilantro	Cantaloupe
Peaches	Zucchini	Dill	Okra
Melons	Eggplant	Basil	Sweet Potatoes
Apples	Cucumbers	Thyme	Arugula
Pears	Corn	Chives	Green Onions
Grapes	Peppers (Bell)	Oregano	Rhubarb
Figs	Beets	Lovage	Dates
Nectarines	Carrots	Marjoram	Lychees
Apricots	Celery	Lavender	Passionfruit
Blackberries	Cabbage	Tarragon	Pawpaws
Elderberries	Potatoes	Rosemary	Raspberries

September

Apples	Broccoli	Sage	Pumpkins
Pears	Carrots	Thyme	Grapes
Grapes	Cauliflower	Rosemary	Cranberries
Plums	Spinach	Parsley	Brussels Sprouts
Figs	Brussels Sprouts	Lavender	Dates
Pawpaws	Beets	Oregano	Artichokes
Persimmons	Butternut Squash	Tarragon	Turnips
Cranberries	Swiss Chard	Chives	Sweet Potatoes
Pomegranates	Kale	Cilantro	Acorn Squash
Kiwi	Arugula	Lemon Balm	Bell Pepper
Quince	Radishes	Marjoram	Chaoterelle
Mangoes	Potatoes	Lemongrass	Napa Cabbage

Contents

Contents

Contents

Breakfast & Sweet Treats

Acai Bowl

SERVES: 1   PREP TIME: 5 MIN   COOK TIME: 0 MIN

Instructions

1. In a blender, combine the frozen acai puree, frozen mixed berries, almond milk, and ripe banana.
2. Blend until smooth and creamy. If needed, add more almond milk to help with blending.
3. Pour the acai smoothie into a bowl.
4. Top the smoothie with granola and sliced fresh fruits.
5. Enjoy your vibrant and refreshing acai bowl!

Tips:
- Boost the nutritional value by adding a tbsp of chia seeds or a scoop of plant-based protein powder to the smoothie.
- Get creative with toppings, such as coconut flakes, cacao nibs, or a drizzle of almond butter.

Ingredients

- 2 packs of frozen acai puree (100g each) - alternatively 200g frozen blueberries or other fruit of choice
- 1 cup frozen mixed berries (e.g., strawberries, blueberries)
- 1/2 cup almond milk
- 1 ripe banana
- Granola
- Sliced fresh fruits (e.g., berries, kiwi, banana)

Tropical Smoothie Bowl
with Fresh Fruit

SERVES: 1   PREP TIME: 10 MIN   COOK TIME: 30 - 35 MIN

Instructions

1. In a blender, combine the frozen bananas, mango chunks, pineapple chunks, and coconut milk.
2. Blend until smooth and creamy, adding more coconut milk if needed to achieve your desired consistency.
3. Pour the smoothie into a bowl.
4. Top the smoothie with granola, sliced fresh fruits, and shredded coconut.
5. Serve immediately and enjoy!

Tips:
- For added protein and nutrients, consider adding a scoop of plant-based protein powder or a handful of spinach to the smoothie.
- Customize the toppings to your preference with ingredients like chia seeds, hemp hearts, or nut butter.

Ingredients

- 2 frozen bananas
- 1 cup mango chunks
- 1/2 cup pineapple chunks
- 1 cup coconut milk
- Granola
- Sliced fresh fruits (e.g., strawberries, kiwi, pineapple)
- Shredded coconut

Chia Seed Pudding
with Fresh Fruit

SERVES: 1   PREP TIME: 5 MIN   CHILL TIME: 4H - OVERNIGHT

Instructions

1. In a bowl, combine the chia seeds, almond milk, and maple syrup (or agave).
2. Stir well to ensure the chia seeds are evenly distributed.
3. Cover the bowl and refrigerate for at least 4 hours or preferably overnight. The chia seeds will absorb the liquid and form a pudding-like consistency.
4. Before serving, give the pudding a good stir to break up any clumps.
5. Top the chia seed pudding with fresh berries and chopped nuts.
6. Enjoy this delicious and nutritious breakfast!

Tips:
- Adjust the sweetness level by adding more or less maple syrup/agave according to your taste.
- If the pudding is too thick, you can thin it out by adding more almond milk.

Ingredients

- 1/4 cup chia seeds
- 1 cup almond milk (or any plant-based milk of your choice)
- 1 tbsp maple syrup or agave syrup
- Fresh berries
- Chopped nuts (e.g., almonds, walnuts)

Raspberry Chia Pudding Parfait

SERVES: 4 | PREP TIME: 5 MIN | CHILL TIME: 2H - OVERNIGHT

Instructions

1. In a mixing bowl, whisk together the chia seeds, almond milk, plant yogurt, maple syrup (or agave syrup), and vanilla extract until well combined.
2. Let the chia seed mixture sit for a few minutes, then whisk again to avoid clumps.
3. Cover the bowl and refrigerate the chia seed mixture for at least 2 hours or preferably overnight to allow it to thicken.
4. Once the chia pudding has reached the desired consistency, give it a stir to break up any remaining clumps.
5. In serving glasses or bowls, layer the chia pudding with fresh or thawed raspberries and granola.
6. Repeat the layers until you fill the glasses or bowls.
7. Garnish the raspberry chia pudding parfait with fresh mint leaves before serving.

Ingredients

- 1/2 cup chia seeds
- 1 cup almond milk (or other plant-based milk)
- 1 cup plant yogurt (coconut, almond, ...)
- 1 tbsp maple syrup or agave syrup
- 1 tsp vanilla extract
- 1 cup fresh or frozen raspberries
- 1/2 cup granola (gluten-free and vegan)
- Fresh mint leaves for garnish

Tips:
- Customize the parfait by using other fruits like strawberries, blueberries, or mangoes.
- To enhance the flavor, you can sprinkle some shredded coconut or cacao nibs between the layers.

Coconut Mango Rice Pudding

SERVES: 2   PREP TIME: 5 MIN   COOK TIME: 25 MIN

Instructions

1. In a large saucepan, combine the arborio rice, coconut milk, almond milk, maple syrup (or agave syrup), vanilla extract, and a pinch of salt.
2. Bring the mixture to a gentle boil over medium heat, then reduce the heat to low and let it simmer, stirring occasionally.
3. Cook the rice pudding for about 20-25 minutes, or until the rice is tender and the pudding has thickened to your desired consistency.
4. Stir in the diced mango during the last few minutes of cooking, reserving some for topping if desired.
5. Remove the rice pudding from the heat and let it cool slightly.
6. Serve the coconut mango rice pudding warm or chilled, and top with toasted coconut flakes and additional diced mango if desired.

Tips:
- For a creamier pudding, you can add a splash of coconut cream or more coconut milk.
- Sprinkle some ground cinnamon or cardamom on top for extra flavor and aroma.

Ingredients

- 1 cup arborio rice
- 1 can (13.5 oz) full-fat coconut milk
- 2 cups almond milk (or other plant-based milk)
- 1/4 cup maple syrup or agave syrup
- 1 tsp vanilla extract
- Pinch of salt
- 1 ripe mango (diced)
- Toasted coconut flakes for topping

Overnight Oats
with Fresh Fruit

SERVES: 1 | PREP TIME: 5 MIN | COOK TIME: OVERNIGHT

Instructions

1. In a jar or airtight container, combine the rolled oats, chia seeds, almond milk, and maple syrup (or agave).
2. Stir well to ensure all ingredients are evenly mixed.
3. Cover the jar and refrigerate it overnight or for at least 8 hours.
4. In the morning, give the overnight oats a good stir to combine everything.
5. Top the oats with fresh berries and sliced bananas.
6. Enjoy the creamy and nutritious breakfast!

Tips:
- If the oats are too thick in the morning, you can add a splash of almond milk to achieve your preferred consistency.
- Experiment with different toppings, such as shredded coconut, nuts, coconut yogurt or a dollop of almond butter.

Ingredients

- 1 cup rolled oats (gluten-free)
- 2 tbsps chia seeds
- 1 1/2 cups almond milk
- 1 tbsp maple syrup or agave syrup
- Fresh berries and sliced bananas for topping

Overnight Oats
with Tropical Fruit

SERVES: 2   PREP TIME: 10 MIN   COOK TIME: OVERNIGHT

Instructions

1. In a mixing bowl or a jar, combine the rolled oats, unsweetened coconut milk, diced fresh mango, diced fresh pineapple, diced fresh papaya, chia seeds, and maple syrup or agave syrup.
2. Stir all the ingredients until well combined.
3. Cover the bowl or jar with a lid or plastic wrap and refrigerate it overnight or for at least 4-6 hours to allow the oats to absorb the liquid and soften.
4. Before serving, give the overnight oats a good stir to mix the ingredients thoroughly.
5. Divide the tropical overnight oats into serving bowls.
6. Optionally, top each bowl with shredded coconut and chopped nuts for extra flavor and crunch.

Tips:
- Feel free to add other favorite tropical fruits like kiwi, passion fruit, or banana to the overnight oats for variety and taste.
- You can also mix in some unsweetened coconut flakes or diced dried tropical fruits for added texture and flavor.
- Prepare a batch of these summer overnight oats ahead of time to have a quick and delicious breakfast ready to enjoy on busy mornings during the summer season.

Ingredients

- 1 cup rolled oats (gluten-free if needed)
- 1 cup unsweetened coconut milk (or any plant-based milk)
- 1/2 cup diced fresh mango
- 1/2 cup diced fresh pineapple
- 1/4 cup diced fresh papaya
- 1 tbsp chia seeds
- 1 tbsp shredded coconut (optional, for topping)
- 1 tbsp chopped nuts (e.g., almonds, walnuts) (optional, for topping)
- 1 tbsp maple syrup or agave syrup (adjust sweetness to taste)

Quinoa Breakfast Bowl

SERVES: 1   PREP TIME: 5 MIN   COOK TIME: 15 MIN

Instructions

1. Rinse the quinoa thoroughly under cold water to remove any bitterness.
2. In a saucepan, combine the rinsed quinoa, almond milk, cinnamon, and vanilla extract.
3. Bring the mixture to a boil over medium-high heat.
4. Once it starts boiling, reduce the heat to low, cover the saucepan, and simmer for about 15 minutes or until the quinoa is cooked and the liquid is absorbed.
5. Fluff the quinoa with a fork.
6. Serve the quinoa in bowls and top with fresh berries and sliced almonds.
7. Add a splash of almond milk if desired, and enjoy your nutritious quinoa breakfast bowl!

Tips:
- For extra creaminess, you can use coconut milk instead of almond milk.
- Sweeten the quinoa with a drizzle of maple syrup or agave if desired.

Ingredients

- cup quinoa
- 2 cups almond milk
- 1 tsp cinnamon
- 1 tsp vanilla extract
- Fresh berries (e.g., blueberries, raspberries)
- Sliced almonds

Banana Pancakes

SERVES: 8 - 10 PANCAKES   PREP TIME: 10 MIN   COOK TIME: 15 MIN

Instructions

1. In a large mixing bowl, mash the ripe bananas with a fork until smooth.
2. Add the almond milk to the mashed bananas and mix well.
3. In a separate bowl, whisk together the gluten-free flour, baking powder, and pinch of cinnamon.
4. Gradually add the dry ingredients to the wet ingredients, stirring until just combined. Be careful not to overmix; a few lumps are okay.
5. Heat a non-stick pan or griddle over medium heat and lightly grease it with oil or cooking spray.
6. Pour a 1/4 cup of the pancake batter onto the hot pan for each pancake.
7. Cook for about 2-3 minutes on each side, or until bubbles form on the surface and the edges look set.
8. Flip the pancakes and cook for an additional 1-2 minutes until they are cooked through and lightly golden.
9. Remove the pancakes from the pan and keep them warm while you cook the remaining batter.
10. Serve the pancakes with your favorite toppings, such as fresh berries, sliced bananas, chopped nuts, vegan whip or a drizzle of maple syrup.

Ingredients

- 2 ripe bananas (mashed)
- 1 cup almond milk
- 1 cup gluten-free flour
- 1 tsp baking powder
- Pinch of cinnamon

Tips:
- If you like a fluffier texture, you can add 1/2 tsp of baking soda to the dry ingredients.
- To prevent sticking, wipe the pan with a paper towel between batches and add a little more oil or cooking spray.

Blueberry Lemon Pancakes

SERVES: 8-10 PANCAKES   PREP TIME: 10 MIN   COOK TIME: 15 MIN

Instructions

1. In a large mixing bowl, whisk together the gluten-free flour blend, coconut sugar, baking powder, and salt.
2. In a separate bowl, mix the unsweetened almond milk, lemon juice, lemon zest, and vanilla extract.
3. Add the wet ingredients to the dry ingredients and stir until just combined. The batter should be slightly lumpy; avoid overmixing.
4. Gently fold in the fresh blueberries into the batter.
5. Preheat a non-stick skillet or griddle over medium heat. Lightly grease the surface with coconut oil or any oil of your choice.
6. Pour about 1/4 cup of pancake batter onto the hot skillet for each pancake.
7. Cook the pancakes for 2-3 minutes on one side, or until bubbles form on the surface and the edges start to look set.
8. Flip the pancakes and cook for an additional 1-2 minutes on the other side, or until they are golden brown.
9. Transfer to a plate, keep them warm by covering them with a clean kitchen towel while you cook the remaining batter.
10. Serve the summery blueberry lemon pancakes with a drizzle of maple syrup and some extra fresh blueberries on top.

Tips:
- To keep the pancakes warm while serving a large batch, preheat your oven to the lowest setting, and place the cooked pancakes on a baking sheet in the oven until ready to serve

Ingredients

- 1 cup gluten-free all-purpose flour blend
- 2 tbsps coconut sugar (or any granulated sweetener)
- 2 tsps baking powder
- 1/4 tsp salt
- 1 cup almond milk (or any plant-based milk)
- 2 tbsps lemon juice
- 1 tbsp lemon zest
- 1 tsp vanilla extract
- 1 cup fresh blueberries
- Coconut oil for cooking
- Maple syrup and additional blueberries for serving

Blueberry Waffles

Instructions

1. In a large mixing bowl, whisk together the all-purpose flour, sugar, baking powder, and salt.
2. In a separate bowl, mix the almond milk, unsweetened applesauce, melted coconut oil, and vanilla extract until well combined.
3. Pour the wet ingredients into the dry ingredients and mix until just combined. Be careful not to overmix; some lumps are okay.
4. Gently fold in the fresh blueberries into the waffle batter.
5. Preheat your waffle maker according to its instructions.
6. Pour the waffle batter onto the hot waffle maker, spreading it out to cover the surface.
7. Close the waffle maker and cook the waffle until it becomes golden brown and crispy.
8. Repeat with the remaining batter to make more waffles.
9. Serve the vegan blueberry waffles with maple syrup, additional fresh blueberries, and a dollop of vegan whipped cream or yogurt.

Tips:
- If you prefer a thicker waffle, reduce the amount of almond milk slightly.
- Top the waffles with chopped nuts or coconut flakes for added texture and flavor.

Ingredients

- 1 1/2 cups gluten-free flour blend
- 2 tbsps sugar
- 2 tsps baking powder
- 1/4 tsp salt
- 1 1/4 cups almond milk (or any plant-based milk)
- 1/4 cup unsweetened applesauce
- 2 tbsps melted coconut oil (or any vegetable oil)
- 1 tsp vanilla extract
- 1/2 cup fresh blueberries

Lemon Poppy Seed Waffles

Instructions

1. In a large mixing bowl, whisk together the gluten-free all-purpose flour, poppy seeds, baking powder, salt, and lemon zest.
2. In a separate bowl, combine the almond milk, melted coconut oil, pure maple syrup or agave syrup, pure vanilla extract, and lemon juice.
3. Pour the wet ingredients into the dry ingredients and mix until just combined. Be careful not to overmix; a few lumps are fine.
4. Preheat your waffle iron.
5. Once the waffle iron is hot, spray or brush it with a little oil to prevent sticking.
6. Pour the waffle batter onto the center of the waffle iron and spread it out slightly using a spoon.
7. Close the waffle iron and cook the waffles until golden brown and crispy.
8. Carefully remove the waffles from the iron and place them on a wire rack to cool slightly.

Tips:
- Top your Lemon Poppy Seed Waffles with a dusting of powdered sugar and fresh berries for a refreshing and delightful summer treat, or some plant-based yogurt for an additional boost of flavor.
- If you prefer a tangier flavor, add more lemon juice to the waffle batter.

Ingredients

- 1 1/2 cups gluten-free all-purpose flour
- 2 tbsps poppy seeds
- 1 tbsp baking powder
- 1/4 tsp salt
- Zest of 1 large lemon
- 1 1/2 cups almond milk or any other plant-based milk
- 2 tbsps melted coconut oil or vegetable oil
- 2 tbsps pure maple syrup or agave syrup
- 1 tsp pure vanilla extract
- Juice of 1 large lemon

Buckwheat Banana Muffins

SERVES: 6 MUFFINS   PREP TIME: 10 MIN   BAKE TIME: 20-25 MIN

Instructions

1. Preheat your oven to 350°F (175°C) and line a muffin tin with paper liners.
2. In a large mixing bowl, whisk together the buckwheat flour, baking powder, baking soda, and salt.
3. In a separate bowl, mash the ripe bananas with a fork until smooth.
4. Add the maple syrup, almond milk, and vanilla extract to the mashed bananas, and stir until well combined.
5. Pour the wet ingredients into the dry ingredients and mix until just combined.
6. If using, fold in the crushed nuts and chocolate chips
7. Spoon the muffin batter into the prepared muffin tin, filling each cup about two-thirds full.
8. Bake in the preheated oven for 20-25 minutes or until a toothpick inserted into the center of a muffin comes out clean.
9. Allow the muffins to cool in the tin for a few minutes before transferring them to a wire rack to cool completely.

Ingredients

- 1 cup buckwheat flour
- 1 tsp baking powder
- 1/2 tsp baking soda
- 1/4 tsp salt
- 3 ripe bananas (mashed)
- 1/4 cup maple syrup or agave syrup
- 1/4 cup almond milk
- 1 tsp vanilla extract
- Handful of crushed nuts an chocolate chips (optional)

Tips:

- For added sweetness, sprinkle a little coconut sugar on top of the muffins before baking.
- Store the muffins in an airtight container for up to 3-4 days or freeze them for later enjoyment.

Chocolate Muffins
with Chocolate Chips

SERVES: 12 MUFFINS   PREP TIME: 15 MIN   BAKE TIME: 20 - 22 MIN

Instructions

1. Preheat your oven to 350°F (175°C). Line a muffin tin with paper liners or grease the cups with oil.
2. In a large mixing bowl, whisk together the all-purpose flour, unsweetened cocoa powder, baking powder, baking soda, and salt.
3. In a separate bowl, mix the almond milk, coconut sugar, melted coconut oil, and vanilla extract until well combined.
4. Pour the wet ingredients into the dry ingredients and stir until just combined. Be careful not to overmix; some lumps are okay.
5. Gently fold in the vegan chocolate chips into the muffin batter.
6. Divide the batter evenly among the muffin cups, filling each cup about two-thirds full.
7. Bake in the preheated oven for 20 to 22 minutes, or until a toothpick inserted into the center of a muffin comes out clean or with just a few moist crumbs.
8. Remove the muffins from the oven and let them cool in the muffin tin for about 5 minutes before transferring them to a wire rack to cool completely.

Ingredients

- 1 1/2 cups gluten-free all-purpose flour blend
- 1/2 cup unsweetened cocoa powder
- 1 tsp baking powder
- 1/2 tsp baking soda
- 1/4 tsp salt
- 1 cup almond milk (or any plant-based milk)
- 1/2 cup coconut sugar (or any granulated sweetener of your choice)
- 1/4 cup melted coconut oil (or any vegetable oil)
- 1 tsp vanilla extract
- 1/2 cup vegan chocolate chips

Tips:
- Feel free to add chopped nuts or coconut flakes for extra texture and flavor.
- For a more indulgent treat, drizzle melted vegan chocolate over the cooled muffins.

Banana Bread
with Chocolate Chips and Nuts

SERVES: 1 LOAF   PREP TIME: 15 MIN   BAKE TIME: 55 - 60 MIN

Instructions

1. Preheat your oven to 350°F (175°C). Grease a 9x5-inch loaf pan and line it with parchment paper.
2. In a large mixing bowl, whisk together the gluten-free all-purpose flour blend, baking powder, baking soda, salt, and ground cinnamon.
3. In a separate bowl, mix the mashed bananas, coconut sugar, melted coconut oil, unsweetened applesauce, and vanilla extract until well combined.
4. Add the wet ingredients to the dry ingredients and stir until just combined. Be careful not to overmix; some lumps are okay.
5. Fold in the chopped nuts and chocolate into the batter.
6. Pour the batter into the loaf pan, spreading it out evenly.
7. Bake in the preheated oven for 55 to 60 minutes, or until a toothpick inserted into the center comes out clean.
8. Remove the banana bread from the oven and let it cool in the pan for about 10 minutes.
9. Carefully transfer the banana bread to a wire rack to cool completely before slicing.

Tips:
- Make sure your bananas are ripe, with brown spots, for the best flavor and sweetness.
- If the top of the banana bread starts to brown too quickly during baking, you can cover it loosely with aluminum foil for the remaining bake time.

Ingredients

- 2 cups gluten-free all-purpose flour blend
- 1 tsp baking powder
- 1/2 tsp baking soda
- 1/4 tsp salt
- 1 tsp ground cinnamon
- 3 ripe bananas, mashed
- 1/2 cup coconut sugar (or any granulated sweetener of your choice)
- 1/4 cup melted coconut oil (or any vegetable oil)
- 1/4 cup unsweetened applesauce
- 1 tsp vanilla extract
- 1/2 cup chopped walnuts, pecans or chocolate chips (optional)

Strawberry Shortcake
with Strawberry Filling

SERVES: 4　　　　PREP TIME: 20 MIN　　　　BAKE TIME: 15 - 18 MIN

Instructions

1. Preheat your oven to 425°F (220°C). Line a baking sheet with parchment paper.
2. In a large mixing bowl, whisk together the gluten-free flour blend, coconut sugar, baking powder, and salt.
3. Add the solid coconut oil to the dry ingredients. Use a pastry cutter or fork to cut the coconut oil into the flour until it resembles coarse crumbs.
4. Stir in the unsweetened almond milk and vanilla extract until a soft dough forms.
5. Drop spoonfuls of the dough onto the prepared baking sheet to make 4 shortcakes.
6. Bake for 15-18 minutes or until lightly golden.
7. While the shortcakes are baking, prepare the strawberry filling by mixing the sliced strawberries with maple syrup.
8. Once the shortcakes are done, let them cool for a few minutes on a wire rack.
9. To serve, slice each shortcake in half horizontally. Spoon some of the strawberry filling onto the bottom half, and top with vegan whipped cream. Place the top half of the shortcake on top.
10. Serve the delightful vegan strawberry shortcake immediately.

Tips:
- Use other fresh fruits like peaches or mixed berries for a variety of flavors.

Ingredients

For the shortcakes:
- 2 cups gluten-free all-purpose flour blend
- 1/4 cup coconut sugar (or any granulated sweetener of your choice)
- 1 tbsp baking powder
- 1/4 tsp salt
- 1/2 cup coconut oil (solid state)
- 3/4 cup unsweetened almond milk (or any plant-based milk)
- 1 tsp vanilla extract

For the strawberry filling:
- 2 cups fresh strawberries, sliced
- 2 tbsps maple syrup or agave syrup

Vegan whipped cream (for serving)

Lemon Blueberry Crumble

SERVES: 4   PREP TIME: 15 MIN   BAKE TIME: 25 - 30 MIN

Instructions

1. Preheat your oven to 350°F (175°C) and lightly grease a baking dish with coconut oil.
2. In a mixing bowl, combine the fresh blueberries, lemon juice, lemon zest, and 1 tbsp of coconut sugar or maple syrup. Toss gently to coat the blueberries, then transfer them to the greased baking dish, spreading them out evenly.
3. In the same mixing bowl, combine the gluten-free rolled oats, almond flour, melted coconut oil, chopped almonds or walnuts (if using), the remaining coconut sugar or maple syrup, and a pinch of salt. Mix until the crumble topping is well combined and clumpy.
4. Spread the crumble mixture evenly over the blueberries in the baking dish.
5. Bake in the preheated oven for 25-30 minutes or until the crumble topping turns golden brown and the blueberries are bubbling underneath.
6. Remove from the oven and let it cool for a few minutes before serving.

Tips:
- Feel free to top it with a scoop of dairy-free vanilla ice cream.

Ingredients

- 2 cups fresh blueberries
- 2 tbsps lemon juice
- 1 tbsp lemon zest
- 1/4 cup coconut sugar or maple syrup
- 1 cup gluten-free rolled oats
- 1/2 cup almond flour
- 1/4 cup coconut oil, melted
- 1/4 cup chopped almonds or walnuts (optional)
- Pinch of salt

Energy Bites with Shredded Coconut

SERVES: 12 - 15 BITES   PREP TIME: 15 MIN   CHILL TIME: 30 - 40 MIN

Instructions

1. In a large mixing bowl, combine the gluten-free rolled oats, almond butter, ground flaxseed, agave syrup (or maple syrup), and vanilla extract. Stir well until all the ingredients are evenly mixed.
2. Add 1/2 cup of shredded coconut into the mixture and continue stirring until the coconut is well distributed and the mixture becomes sticky and easily moldable.
3. Place the mixture in the refrigerator for about 15-20 minutes to firm up slightly, which will make it easier to shape.
4. Meanwhile, spread the remaining 1/2 cup of shredded coconut on a small plate or flat surface.
5. Once the mixture has chilled, take small portions and roll them into bite-sized balls using your hands.
6. Roll each energy bite in the shredded coconut on the plate, coating the surface evenly.
7. Place the coated energy bites on a parchment-lined tray or plate and refrigerate for at least 30 minutes to set completely.
8. Once set, transfer the energy bites to an airtight container and store them in the refrigerator for up to one week.

Ingredients

- 1 cup gluten-free rolled oats
- 1/2 cup almond butter
- 1/4 cup ground flaxseed
- 1/4 cup agave syrup or maple syrup
- 1 tsp vanilla extract
- 1/2 cup unsweetened shredded coconut (for the mixture)
- 1/2 cup unsweetened shredded coconut (for coating)

Tips:
- If the mixture is too dry to form into balls, add a little more almond butter or agave syrup to achieve the desired consistency.
- Feel free to swap almond butter with other nut or seed butters, such as peanut butter or sunflower seed butter, according to your preference.

Chocolate Avocado Mousse

SERVES: 4   PREP TIME: 10 MIN   CHILL TIME: 1 HOUR

Instructions

1. Cut the avocados in half, remove the pits, and scoop the flesh into a blender or food processor.
2. Add the unsweetened cocoa powder, maple syrup (or agave syrup), almond milk, vanilla extract, and a pinch of salt to the blender.
3. Blend all the ingredients until you achieve a smooth and creamy mousse consistency.
4. Taste the mousse and adjust the sweetness or cocoa level according to your preference.
5. Transfer the chocolate avocado mousse to individual serving dishes or a large bowl.
6. Chill the mousse in the refrigerator for at least 1 hour before serving.
7. Garnish with fresh berries and some vegan whipped cream if desired.

Ingredients

- 2 ripe avocados
- 1/4 cup unsweetened cocoa powder
- 1/4 cup maple syrup or agave syrup
- 1/4 cup almond milk
- 1 tsp vanilla extract
- Pinch of salt
- Fresh berries for topping (optional)

Tips:
- For a nutty flavor, you can use hazelnut milk instead of almond milk.
- Create a chocolate-orange mousse by adding a splash of orange juice and some orange zest to the mixture.

Coconut Lime Panna Cotta

SERVES: 4   PREP TIME: 10 MIN   CHILL TIME: 2 - 3 HOURS

Instructions

1. In a saucepan, combine the coconut milk, fresh lime juice, pure maple syrup or agave syrup, and vanilla extract. Heat the mixture over medium-low heat, stirring occasionally, until well combined. Do not bring it to a boil.
2. In a separate small bowl, mix the water and agar agar powder until it dissolves completely.
3. Add the agar agar mixture to the coconut milk mixture and stir continuously for about 2-3 minutes to ensure it's well incorporated.
4. Continue cooking the mixture for another 3-4 minutes until it starts to thicken slightly.
5. Remove the saucepan from the heat and let the mixture cool for a few minutes.
6. Pour the coconut lime mixture into individual serving glasses or ramekins.
7. Chill the Panna Cotta in the refrigerator for at least 2-3 hours or until set.
8. Before serving, garnish each Panna Cotta with lime zest.

Ingredients

- 1 can (14 oz) full-fat coconut milk
- 1/4 cup fresh lime juice
- 1/4 cup pure maple syrup or agave syrup
- 1 tsp vanilla extract
- 1/4 cup water
- 1 tbsp agar agar powder
- Zest of 1 lime for garnish

Tips:
- For a more intense lime flavor, you can add more lime juice or adjust the amount of lime zest according to your preference.
- To unmold the Panna Cotta easily, you can lightly grease the serving glasses or ramekins with a little coconut oil before pouring in the mixture.
- Serve the Coconut Lime Panna Cotta with a drizzle of raspberry or strawberry sauce for a delightful burst of fruity goodness.

Smoothies, Drinks & Ice Cream

Green Protein Smoothie

Instructions

1. In a blender, combine the spinach, kale, avocado, cucumber, green apple, vanilla protein and coconut water.
2. Blend until smooth and well combined.
3. Taste and adjust the sweetness by adding a little agave syrup or honey if desired.
4. Pour the green smoothie into glasses and serve immediately.

Tips:
- To make the smoothie colder and more refreshing, you can add a handful of ice cubes before blending.
- For added creaminess and nutrition, include a couple tbsp of coconut yogurt or a ripe banana in the smoothie.

Ingredients

- 1/2 cup spinach
- 1/2 cup kale
- 1/2 avocado
- 1/2 cucumber (peeled and chopped)
- 1 green apple (cored and chopped)
- 1 cup coconut water
- 1 scoop vanilla plant protein (or any other protein powder of choice)

Watermelon Smoothie

SERVES: 2   PREP TIME: 10 MIN   COOK TIME: 0 MIN

Instructions

1. In a blender, add the fresh watermelon cubes, unsweetened coconut milk, fresh lime juice, and chia seeds (if using).
2. Optionally, add a few ice cubes to the blender if you prefer a colder and thicker smoothie.
3. Blend all the ingredients until smooth and creamy, scraping down the sides of the blender as needed.
4. Taste the smoothie and adjust sweetness if desired by adding agave syrup or maple syrup.
5. Pour the refreshing vegan gluten-free watermelon smoothie into glasses.
6. Optionally, garnish with a small watermelon slice or a fresh mint sprig for presentation.

Tips:
- This simple watermelon smoothie showcases the natural sweetness and freshness of the watermelon, making it a perfect summer treat.
- For a thinner consistency, you can add more coconut milk or water to the smoothie.
- Chia seeds add a boost of fiber, protein, and omega-3 fatty acids, but you can omit them if you prefer a smoother texture.

Ingredients

- 3 cups fresh watermelon, cubed and deseeded
- 1/2 cup unsweetened coconut milk (or any plant-based milk)
- 1 tbsp fresh lime juice
- 1 tbsp chia seeds (optional, for added nutrition and texture)
- 1-2 tsps agave syrup or maple syrup (adjust sweetness to taste)
- Ice cubes (optional, for a colder and thicker smoothie)

Mango Lassi

Instructions

1. In a blender, add the diced ripe mangoes, unsweetened coconut yogurt, unsweetened almond milk, maple syrup, ground cardamom, and a pinch of ground turmeric.
2. If you prefer a colder and thicker lassi, you can also add a few ice cubes to the blender.
3. Blend all the ingredients until smooth and creamy, scraping down the sides of the blender as needed.
4. Taste the mango lassi and adjust sweetness if desired by adding more agave syrup or maple syrup.
5. Pour the vegan gluten-free mango lassi into glasses.
6. Optionally, garnish with fresh mint leaves or sliced almonds for presentation.

Ingredients

- 2 ripe mangoes, peeled and diced (or 2 cups frozen mango chunks)
- 1 cup coconut yogurt (or any other plant-based yogurt)
- 1 cup almond milk (or any other plant-based milk)
- 2 tbsps maple syrup
- 1/2 tsp ground cardamom (optional)
- A pinch of ground turmeric (optional)
- Ice cubes (optional, for a colder and thicker lassi)
- Fresh mint leaves or sliced almonds for garnish (optional)

Tips:
- If fresh ripe mangoes are not available, you can use frozen mango chunks. Just make sure they are thawed before blending.
- For a richer and creamier lassi, you can add a tbsp of coconut cream or cashew butter to the blender.
- Feel free to customize the lassi by adding a pinch of ground cinnamon or ground ginger for different flavor variations.
- This mango lassi is best served fresh, but you can refrigerate any leftovers for a few hours. Give it a quick stir before serving if it separates. Enjoy the lassi as a refreshing drink or a tasty dessert!

Raspberry Lime Smoothie

SERVES: 1 - 2   PREP TIME: 5 MIN   COOK TIME: 0 MIN

Instructions

1. In a blender, combine the frozen raspberries, ripe banana, unsweetened almond milk, lime juice, chia seeds, almond butter or cashew butter, and pure maple syrup (if using).
2. Blend until the mixture is smooth and creamy. If you prefer a thicker consistency, you can add a few ice cubes and blend again until well combined.
3. Taste the smoothie and adjust sweetness or tanginess to your liking by adding more maple syrup or lime juice if desired.
4. Pour the raspberry lime smoothie into glasses and serve immediately.

Tips:

- To make this smoothie even more refreshing, add a small handful of fresh mint leaves to the blender and blend them with the other ingredients. Mint complements the raspberry and lime flavors wonderfully.
- For an extra nutritional boost, consider adding a spoonful of hemp seeds or flax seeds to the smoothie. These seeds are rich in omega-3 fatty acids and provide a nutty flavor that complements the raspberry lime combination.

Ingredients

- 1 cup frozen raspberries
- 1 ripe banana
- 1 cup unsweetened almond milk (or any plant-based milk of your choice)
- Juice of 1 lime
- 1 tbsp chia seeds
- 1 tbsp almond butter or cashew butter
- 1 tbsp pure maple syrup (optional, for added sweetness)
- Ice cubes (optional, for a chilled smoothie)

Iced Coffee Smoothie

SERVES: 1 - 2   PREP TIME: 5 MIN   COOK TIME: 0 MIN

Instructions

1. Brew your favorite coffee and let it cool to room temperature or refrigerate for a few hours.
2. In a blender, combine the cooled coffee, ripe banana, unsweetened almond milk, almond butter or cashew butter, pure maple syrup or agave syrup, and pure vanilla extract.
3. Blend until the mixture is smooth and creamy.
4. Taste the iced coffee smoothie and adjust sweetness to your liking by adding more maple syrup or agave syrup if desired.
5. Add ice cubes to the blender and blend again until the smoothie is chilled and frothy.
6. Pour the iced coffee smoothie into glasses and serve with vegan whip if desired.

Tips:
- To make it even more indulgent, add a splash of dairy-free creamer or coconut milk to the iced coffee smoothie. It will enhance the creaminess and create a luxurious texture.
- For a mocha twist, add a tbsp of unsweetened cocoa powder to the blender along with the other ingredients.

Ingredients

- 1 cup brewed coffee, cooled (use your favorite coffee or decaf for a caffeine-free option)
- 1 ripe banana
- 1 cup unsweetened almond milk (or any plant-based milk of your choice)
- 1 tbsp almond butter or cashew butter
- 1 tbsp pure maple syrup or agave syrup
- 1/2 tsp pure vanilla extract
- Ice cubes
- vegan whipped cream (optional)

Blueberry Almond Smoothie

Instructions

1. In a blender, combine the frozen blueberries, ripe banana, unsweetened almond milk, almond butter, chia seeds, and pure maple syrup (if using).
2. Blend until the mixture is smooth and creamy. If you prefer a thicker consistency, you can add a few ice cubes and blend again until well combined.
3. Taste the smoothie and adjust sweetness to your liking by adding more maple syrup if desired.
4. Pour the blueberry almond smoothie into glasses and serve immediately.

Tips:
- To make the smoothie even more nutritious, consider adding a handful of fresh spinach or kale to the blender. The mild taste of these leafy greens will not overpower the blueberry and almond flavors but will add extra vitamins and minerals to your smoothie.
- For a protein boost, add a scoop of your favorite plant-based protein powder to the smoothie. This is especially beneficial if you're having the smoothie as a post-workout treat or a quick breakfast.

Ingredients

- 1 cup frozen blueberries
- 1 ripe banana
- 1 cup unsweetened almond milk (or any plant-based milk of your choice)
- 2 tbsps almond butter
- 1 tbsp chia seeds
- 1 tbsp pure maple syrup (optional, for added sweetness)
- Ice cubes (optional, for a chilled smoothie)

Iced Matcha Latte

Instructions

1. In a glass, whisk the matcha green tea powder with a small amount of cold water until it forms a smooth paste.
2. Add the unsweetened almond milk and pure maple syrup or agave syrup to the glass.
3. Stir well to combine all the ingredients and taste the iced matcha latte. Adjust sweetness according to your preference.
4. Add ice cubes to the glass to chill the drink further.
5. Stir once more before serving and serve with vegan whipped cream if desired.

Tips:

- For a creamier and frothier latte, you can use a milk frother or a hand blender to froth the almond milk before adding it to the matcha mixture. This will create a cafe-style texture and enhance the overall experience.
- To make a stronger matcha flavor, adjust the amount of matcha powder according to your preference. Start with 1 tsp and add more if desired.

Ingredients

- 1 tsp matcha green tea powder
- 1 cup unsweetened almond milk (or any plant-based milk of your choice)
- 1 tbsp pure maple syrup or agave syrup (adjust to taste)
- Ice cubes
- vegan whipped cream (optional)

Iced Coffee

Instructions

1. In a glass, combine the cooled brewed coffee, unsweetened almond milk, and pure maple syrup or agave syrup.
2. Stir well to combine all the ingredients and taste the iced coffee. Adjust sweetness according to your preference.
3. Add ice cubes to the glass to chill the drink further.
4. Stir once more before serving.

Tips:
- For a bolder coffee flavor, consider using cold-brewed coffee instead of regular brewed coffee. Cold-brewed coffee tends to have a smoother and less bitter taste, perfect for iced coffee drinks.
- To make it even more indulgent, top your iced coffee with a dollop of dairy-free whipped cream and a sprinkle of cocoa powder.

Ingredients

- 1 cup brewed coffee, cooled
- 1 cup unsweetened almond milk (or any plant-based milk of your choice)
- 1 tbsp pure maple syrup or agave syrup (adjust to taste)
- Ice cubes

Iced Chocolate

SERVES: 1 - 2   PREP TIME: 5 MIN   COOK TIME: 0 MIN

Instructions

1. In a glass, whisk together the unsweetened cocoa powder, unsweetened almond milk, pure maple syrup or agave syrup until well combined.
2. Taste the iced chocolate and adjust sweetness according to your liking.
3. Add ice cubes to the glass to chill the drink further.
4. Stir once more before serving.

Tips:
- For a richer chocolate flavor, you can use chocolate-flavored almond milk instead of adding cocoa powder separately.
- Garnish your iced chocolate with dairy-free chocolate shavings or a sprinkle of cinnamon for an extra touch of decadence.

Ingredients

- 2 tbsps unsweetened cocoa powder
- 1 cup unsweetened almond milk (or any plant-based milk of your choice)
- 2 tbsps pure maple syrup or agave syrup (adjust to taste)
- Ice cubes
- vegan whipped cream (optional)

Peach Ginger Iced Tea

SERVES: 4   PREP TIME: 10 MIN   CHILL TIME: 1 HOUR OR MORE

Instructions

1. In a pitcher, combine the sliced peaches, cooled brewed black tea, grated fresh ginger, and pure maple syrup or agave syrup.
2. Stir well to combine all the ingredients and taste the iced tea. Adjust sweetness according to your preference.
3. Chill the peach ginger iced tea in the refrigerator for at least 1 hour to allow the flavors to meld.
4. Add ice cubes to individual glasses and pour the peach ginger iced tea over the ice.
5. Stir once more before serving.

Tips:
- For an extra flavor boost, you can add a splash of peach liqueur or peach schnapps to the pitcher of iced tea.
- To make the iced tea more visually appealing, you can garnish each glass with a peach slice and a sprig of fresh mint.

Ingredients

- 2 ripe peaches, pitted and sliced
- 4 cups brewed black tea, cooled
- 1 tbsp grated fresh ginger
- 2 tbsps pure maple syrup or agave syrup (adjust to taste)
- Ice cubes

Blueberry Lavender Iced Tea

SERVES: 4	PREP TIME: 10 MIN	CHILL TIME: 1 HOUR OR MORE

Instructions

1. In a saucepan, bring the water to a boil. Remove from heat and add the black tea (loose-leaf or tea bags). Let it steep for 5 minutes.
2. After steeping, remove the tea leaves or tea bags from the saucepan.
3. In a separate saucepan, combine the fresh or frozen blueberries and dried lavender flowers with 1 cup of water. Bring to a simmer and let it cook for 5 minutes.
4. Remove the blueberry and lavender mixture from heat and strain it through a fine-mesh sieve into the black tea.
5. Stir in the pure maple syrup or agave syrup and taste the iced tea. Adjust sweetness according to your preference.
6. Let the blueberry lavender iced tea cool to room temperature, then refrigerate for at least 1 hour to chill.
7. Add ice cubes to individual glasses and pour the blueberry lavender iced tea over the ice.
8. Garnish each glass with a fresh lavender sprig and a few blueberries if desired.

Ingredients

- 4 cups water
- 4 tbsps loose-leaf black tea or 4 black tea bags
- 1 cup fresh or frozen blueberries
- 2 tbsps dried lavender flowers
- 2 tbsps pure maple syrup or agave syrup (adjust to taste)
- Ice cubes
- Fresh lavender sprigs and blueberries for garnish (optional)

Tips:
- If you prefer a stronger blueberry flavor, you can increase the amount of blueberries in the recipe or muddle a few blueberries in the glass before pouring the iced tea.
- For an extra floral touch, add a drop of edible lavender essential oil to the blueberry and lavender mixture. Make sure to use food-grade essential oil suitable for consumption.

Pineapple Ginger Iced Tea

SERVES: 4 | PREP TIME: 10 MIN | CHILL TIME: 1 HOUR OR MORE

Instructions

1. In a saucepan, bring the water to a boil. Remove from heat and add the black tea (loose-leaf or tea bags). Let it steep for 5 minutes.
2. After steeping, remove the tea leaves or tea bags from the saucepan.
3. In a blender, combine the fresh pineapple chunks and thinly sliced ginger with 1 cup of water. Blend until smooth.
4. Place a fine-mesh sieve over the saucepan with the black tea and pour the pineapple ginger mixture through the sieve to strain out any pulp.
5. Stir in the pure maple syrup or agave syrup and taste the iced tea. Adjust sweetness according to your preference.
6. Let the pineapple ginger iced tea cool to room temperature, then refrigerate for at least 1 hour to chill.
7. Add ice cubes to individual glasses and pour the pineapple ginger iced tea over the ice.
8. Garnish each glass with pineapple slices and fresh mint leaves if desired.

Ingredients

- 4 cups water
- 4 tbsps loose-leaf black tea or 4 black tea bags
- 1 cup fresh pineapple chunks
- 1-inch piece of fresh ginger, peeled and thinly sliced
- 2 tbsps pure maple syrup or agave syrup (adjust to taste)
- Ice cubes
- Pineapple slices and fresh mint leaves for garnish (optional)

Tips:
- For an extra zesty kick, add a squeeze of fresh lime juice to the iced tea before serving.
- To make it even more tropical, you can add a splash of coconut milk to the pineapple ginger iced tea for a creamy and luscious twist.

Cucumber Mint Lemonade

SERVES: 4   PREP TIME: 15 MIN   CHILL TIME: 1 HOUR OR MORE

Instructions

1. In a blender, combine the sliced cucumbers, lemon juice, fresh mint leaves, and water.
2. Blend until the mixture is well combined and the cucumbers and mint are finely blended.
3. Strain the cucumber mint mixture through a fine-mesh sieve into a pitcher to remove any pulp.
4. Stir in the pure maple syrup or agave syrup and taste the lemonade. Adjust sweetness according to your preference.
5. Chill the cucumber mint lemonade in the refrigerator for at least 1 hour.
6. Add ice cubes to individual glasses and pour the cucumber mint lemonade over the ice.
7. Stir once more before serving.

Ingredients

- 2 medium cucumbers, peeled and sliced
- Juice of 3 lemons
- 1/4 cup fresh mint leaves
- 4 cups water
- 2 tbsps pure maple syrup or agave syrup (adjust to taste)
- Ice cubes

Tips:
- For an extra cooling effect, freeze some cucumber slices in ice cube trays and use them as ice cubes in your lemonade.
- Garnish your cucumber mint lemonade with a sprig of fresh mint and a lemon wheel for a touch of elegance.

Banana Popsicles

Instructions

1. In a blender, combine the ripe bananas, coconut milk, pure maple syrup or agave syrup, pure vanilla extract, and a pinch of salt.
2. Blend until the mixture is smooth and the bananas are fully blended.
3. Taste the mixture and adjust sweetness according to your preference by adding more sweetener if needed.
4. Stir in the unsweetened shredded coconut or chopped nuts into the banana coconut mixture for added texture (optional).
5. Pour the banana coconut mixture into popsicle molds, leaving a little room at the top for expansion.
6. Insert popsicle sticks into each mold.
7. Place the popsicle molds in the freezer and freeze for at least 4 hours or until fully set.

Ingredients

- 2 ripe bananas
- 1 can (13.5 oz) full-fat coconut milk
- 3 tbsps pure maple syrup or agave syrup (adjust to taste)
- 1 tsp pure vanilla extract
- Pinch of salt
- Unsweetened shredded coconut or chopped nuts for added texture (optional)

Tips:
- For an extra creamy and indulgent touch, you can add 1-2 tbsps of unsweetened coconut cream to the banana coconut mixture before pouring it into the popsicle molds.
- To make the popsicles more visually appealing, you can sprinkle a little extra shredded coconut or chopped nuts on top of each popsicle before freezing.

Mango Coconut Popsicles

SERVES: 6 POPSICLES   PREP TIME: 10 MIN   CHILL TIME: 4H OR MORE

Instructions

1. In a blender or food processor, combine the diced mangos, coconut milk, maple syrup (or agave syrup), vanilla extract, and a pinch of salt.
2. Blend the mixture until smooth and creamy.
3. Pour the mango coconut mixture into popsicle molds.
4. Insert popsicle sticks into each mold.
5. Freeze the popsicles for at least 4 hours or until they are completely frozen.
6. Once frozen, remove the popsicles from the molds and enjoy these refreshing vegan mango coconut popsicles on a hot summer day.

Ingredients

- 2 ripe mangos, peeled and diced
- 1 can (13.5 oz) full-fat coconut milk
- 2 tbsps maple syrup or agave syrup
- 1 tsp vanilla extract
- Pinch of salt

Tips:
- For a tropical twist, add a squeeze of lime juice to the mixture before blending.
- You can also add shredded coconut to the popsicle molds for added texture.

Berry Blast Popsicles

SERVES: 6 POPSICLES   PREP TIME: 10 MIN   CHILL TIME: 4H OR MORE

Instructions

1. In a blender, combine the coconut milk, mixed berries, agave syrup, and vanilla extract.
2. Blend until the mixture is smooth and well-combined.
3. Taste the mixture and adjust the sweetness if needed by adding more agave syrup or maple syrup.
4. Pour the mixture into popsicle molds, leaving a little space at the top for expansion.
5. Insert popsicle sticks into each mold.
6. Place the molds in the freezer and freeze for at least 4-6 hours, or until the popsicles are completely frozen.

Ingredients

- 1 cup coconut milk
- 1 cup mixed berries (strawberries, blueberries, raspberries, blackberries)
- 2 tbsps agave syrup or maple syrup
- 1 tsp pure vanilla extract

Tips:

- If you have leftover smoothie mixture, pour it into ice cube trays and freeze. These berry coconut ice cubes are perfect for adding a burst of flavor to your water or other beverages.
- To easily remove the popsicles from the molds, briefly run the molds under warm water to loosen the popsicles before gently pulling them out.

Creamy Chocolate Coconut Popsicles

SERVES: 6 POPSICLES   PREP TIME: 10 MIN   CHILL TIME: 4H OR MORE

Instructions

1. In a mixing bowl, whisk together the full-fat coconut milk, unsweetened cocoa powder, coconut sugar or maple syrup, pure vanilla extract, and a pinch of salt. Ensure the mixture is well combined and smooth.
2. Taste the chocolate coconut mixture and adjust sweetness to your preference by adding more coconut sugar or maple syrup if desired.
3. Pour the mixture into popsicle molds, leaving a little space at the top for expansion while freezing.
4. Insert popsicle sticks into each mold, making sure they are well-positioned.
5. Place the molds in the freezer and freeze for at least 4-6 hours, or until the popsicles are completely frozen.

Ingredients

- 1 can (14 oz) full-fat coconut milk
- 1/4 cup unsweetened cocoa powder
- 1/4 cup coconut sugar or maple syrup
- 1 tsp pure vanilla extract
- Pinch of salt

Tips:
- For added texture and flavor, consider stirring in dairy-free chocolate chips or cacao nibs into the chocolate coconut mixture before pouring it into the popsicle molds. It will add delightful bursts of chocolate goodness as you savor each bite.
- To create a more indulgent version, drizzle melted dairy-free chocolate over the frozen popsicles before serving. It will add a decadent touch and elevate their visual appeal.

Creamy Lemon-Raspberry Popsicles

SERVES: 6 POPSICLES   PREP TIME: 10 MIN   CHILL TIME: 4H OR MORE

Instructions

1. In a blender, combine the unsweetened almond milk, soaked and drained cashews, coconut cream, fresh lemon juice, lemon zest, agave syrup or maple syrup, and a pinch of salt.
2. Blend until the mixture is smooth and creamy, ensuring there are no cashew chunks left.
3. Taste the mixture and adjust sweetness and lemon flavor to your liking by adding more agave syrup or lemon juice if desired.
4. Add the frozen raspberries to the blender and pulse a few times until the raspberries are broken down, leaving some small chunks for texture and visual appeal.
5. Pour the lemon-raspberry mixture into popsicle molds, leaving a little space at the top for expansion while freezing.
6. Insert popsicle sticks into each mold, making sure they are well-positioned.
7. Place the molds in the freezer and freeze for at least 4-6 hours, or until the popsicles are completely frozen.

Ingredients

- 1 cup unsweetened almond milk (or any plant-based milk of your choice)
- 1/4 cup raw cashews (soaked for 4 hours or overnight and drained)
- 1/4 cup coconut cream
- 1/4 cup fresh lemon juice
- 1 tbsp lemon zest
- 1/4 cup agave syrup or maple syrup
- 1 cup frozen raspberries
- Pinch of salt

Tips:
- For added crunch and texture, consider stirring in a handful of crushed almonds or pistachios into the lemon-raspberry mixture before pouring it into the popsicle molds.
- To make these popsicles even more refreshing, add a few fresh mint leaves to the blender and blend them with the mixture for a delightful twist of flavor.

Piña Colada Popsicles

SERVES: 6 POPSICLES   PREP TIME: 10 MIN   CHILL TIME: 4H OR MORE

Instructions

1. In a blender, combine the drained pineapple chunks, full-fat coconut milk, coconut sugar or maple syrup, pure vanilla extract, and a pinch of salt.
2. Blend until the mixture is smooth and creamy, ensuring there are no pineapple fibers left.
3. Taste the piña colada mixture and adjust sweetness to your liking by adding more coconut sugar or maple syrup if desired.
4. Pour the mixture into popsicle molds, leaving a little space at the top for expansion while freezing.
5. Insert popsicle sticks into each mold, making sure they are well-positioned.
6. Place the molds in the freezer and freeze for at least 4-6 hours, or until the popsicles are completely frozen.

Ingredients

- 1 cup canned pineapple chunks, drained
- 1 can (14 oz) full-fat coconut milk
- 2 tbsps coconut sugar or maple syrup
- 1 tsp pure vanilla extract
- Pinch of salt
- Unsweetened shredded coconut (optional, for coating)

Tips:

- If you'd like a fun and delicious twist, you can coat the frozen popsicles with unsweetened shredded coconut before serving. Simply dip each popsicle in water or run it under warm water for a few seconds, then roll it in shredded coconut to create a tropical and visually appealing treat.

Matcha Coconut Popsicles

SERVES: 6 POPSICLES PREP TIME: 10 MIN CHILL TIME: 4H OR MORE

Instructions

1. In a mixing bowl, whisk together the coconut milk, matcha powder, pure maple syrup or agave syrup, pure vanilla extract, and a pinch of salt until well combined.
2. Taste the mixture and adjust sweetness according to your preference by adding more sweetener if needed.
3. Stir in the unsweetened shredded coconut into the matcha coconut mixture for added texture (optional).
4. Pour the matcha coconut mixture into popsicle molds, leaving a little room at the top for expansion.
5. Insert popsicle sticks into each mold.
6. Place the popsicle molds in the freezer and freeze for at least 4 hours or until fully set.

Ingredients

- 1 can (13.5 oz) full-fat coconut milk
- 2 tsps matcha powder
- 3 tbsps pure maple syrup or agave syrup (adjust to taste)
- 1 tsp pure vanilla extract
- Pinch of salt
- Unsweetened shredded coconut for added texture (optional)

Tips:
- For a creamier texture, you can add 1-2 tbsps of unsweetened coconut cream to the matcha coconut mixture before pouring it into the popsicle molds.
- To enhance the matcha flavor, you can dust a little extra matcha powder on top of each popsicle before freezing.

Lunch & Dinner

Avocado on Toast

Instructions

1. Cut the ripe avocado in half, remove the pit, and scoop the flesh into a bowl.
2. Use a fork to mash the avocado until smooth, or leave it slightly chunky if you prefer.
3. Toast the gluten-free bread slices until golden and crispy.
4. Spread the mashed avocado evenly on each toast slice.
5. Top the avocado toast with sliced cherry tomatoes and sprinkle with a pinch of red pepper flakes.
6. Drizzle a little olive oil over the top for added flavor.
7. Serve immediately for a quick and tasty breakfast!

Ingredients

- 1 ripe avocado
- 2 slices of gluten-free bread
- Cherry tomatoes (sliced in halves)
- Pinch of red pepper flakes
- Drizzle of olive oil

Tips:
- Elevate the flavors with a squeeze of fresh lemon juice or a sprinkle of sea salt.
- Add some sliced cucumber or microgreens on top for extra freshness and crunch.

Vegan Omelette
with a Side Salad

SERVES: 1   PREP TIME: 10 MIN   COOK TIME: 15 MIN

Instructions

1. In a bowl, whisk together the chickpea flour, water, turmeric, salt, and pepper until you get a smooth batter.
2. Stir in the diced bell peppers, chopped scallions, and halved cherry tomatoes.
3. Heat the olive oil in a non-stick skillet over medium heat.
4. Pour half of the batter into the skillet and spread it out evenly to form a round shape.
5. Cook the omelette for about 3-4 minutes or until the edges are set and the bottom is golden brown.
6. Flip the omelette carefully using a spatula and cook the other side for an additional 2-3 minutes.
7. Repeat the process with the remaining batter to make a second omelette.
8. Serve the vegan omelettes with a side of salad or your favorite sauce.

Ingredients

- 1 cup chickpea flour
- 1 cup water
- 1/2 cup diced bell peppers
- 1/4 cup chopped scallions
- 1/4 cup cherry tomatoes (halved)
- 1/4 tsp turmeric
- Salt and pepper to taste
- 1 tbsp olive oil

Tips:
- Customize the fillings to your liking by adding sautéed mushrooms, spinach, or vegan cheese.
- Be patient when flipping the omelette to avoid breaking it; you can use a large plate to help with the flipping.

Spinach Artichoke Dip
baked

SERVES: 1 BOWL   PREP TIME: 15 MIN   COOK TIME: 10 MIN

Instructions

1. Preheat the oven to 375°F (190°C).
2. In a high-speed blender or food processor, blend the soaked cashews, olive oil, and a splash of water until you achieve a smooth and creamy consistency. Set aside.
3. In a skillet over medium heat, sauté the diced onion and minced garlic in olive oil until softened and fragrant.
4. Add the spinach to the skillet and cook until wilted.
5. Stir in the chopped artichoke hearts and cook for an additional 2 minutes.
6. In a mixing bowl, combine the sautéed spinach and artichoke mixture with the blended cashews, vegan mayonnaise, nutritional yeast, lemon juice, salt, and black pepper. Mix well.
7. Transfer the mixture to an oven-safe dish and spread it out evenly.
8. Bake in the preheated oven for about 15 minutes, or until the dip is heated through and slightly bubbly.
9. Serve the vegan spinach artichoke dip warm with tortilla chips, pita bread, or veggie sticks for dipping.

Tips:
- For a smoky flavor, you can add a dash of liquid smoke to the dip.
- This dip can be made ahead of time and reheated before serving.

Ingredients

- 1 cup raw cashews (soaked in water for at least 4 hours or overnight)
- 1 tbsp olive oil
- 1 small onion (finely diced)
- 2 cloves garlic (minced)
- 2 cups packed fresh spinach (chopped)
- 1 can artichoke hearts (drained and chopped)
- 1/2 cup vegan mayonnaise
- 1/4 cup nutritional yeast
- 1 tbsp lemon juice
- 1/2 tsp salt
- 1/4 tsp black pepper

Mango Avocado Salsa

SERVES: 4   PREP TIME: 15 MIN   COOK TIME: 0 MIN

Instructions

1. In a mixing bowl, combine the diced mango, diced avocado, chopped red onion, chopped cilantro, and finely chopped jalapeño (if using).
2. Drizzle the lime juice and olive oil over the mixture.
3. Season with salt and pepper to taste.
4. Gently toss all the ingredients together until well combined.
5. Cover the bowl and refrigerate the mango avocado salsa for at least 15-30 minutes to allow the flavors to meld.
6. Once chilled, give the salsa a quick stir and adjust the seasoning if needed.
7. Serve the refreshing mango avocado salsa with gluten-free tortilla chips as a delicious and healthy appetizer.

Tips:
- You can customize the salsa by adding diced cucumber or diced bell peppers for additional crunch and flavor.
- For a sweeter variation, drizzle a little agave syrup or honey over the salsa.
- This salsa can also be used as a topping for grilled tofu or as a garnish for vegan tacos and salads.

Ingredients

- 1 ripe mango, peeled and diced
- 1 ripe avocado, peeled, pitted, and diced
- 1/4 cup red onion, finely chopped
- 1/4 cup fresh cilantro, chopped
- 1 small jalapeño, seeds removed and finely chopped (optional for heat)
- 1 tbsp lime juice
- 1 tbsp olive oil
- Salt and pepper to taste
- Tortilla chips (gluten-free) for serving

Vegan Spring Rolls
with Rice Vinegar Dipping Sauce

SERVES: 8 ROLLS   PREP TIME: 20 MIN   COOK TIME: 0 MIN

Instructions

1. Prepare the rice vermicelli noodles according to the package instructions, then drain and rinse with cold water.
2. Fill a large bowl with warm water. Dip one rice paper wrapper into the water for about 5-10 seconds until it softens.
3. Carefully remove the softened rice paper from the water and lay it flat on a clean, damp kitchen towel.
4. In the center of the rice paper, place a small amount of cooked rice vermicelli noodles, shredded lettuce, cucumber, carrot, mint leaves, and cilantro leaves.
5. Fold the sides of the rice paper over the filling and then tightly roll it up from the bottom, similar to a burrito.
6. Repeat the process for the remaining rice paper wrappers and fillings.
7. To make the dipping sauce, whisk together the soy sauce, rice vinegar, agave syrup, minced garlic, and grated ginger in a small bowl.
8. Serve the spring rolls with the rice vinegar dipping sauce.

Tips:
- For added protein, you can include tofu strips or cooked/roasted/raw tempeh in the spring rolls.
- To prevent the rice paper from sticking to the surface, place a damp paper towel or plastic wrap under the rolls while assembling.

Ingredients

Spring Rolls:
- 8 rice paper wrappers
- 1 cup cooked rice vermicelli noodles
- 1 cup shredded lettuce
- 1/2 cucumber (julienne)
- 1/2 carrot (julienne)
- Fresh mint leaves
- Fresh cilantro leaves

Rice vinegar sauce:
- 3 tbsps soy sauce
- 1 tbsp rice vinegar
- 1 tbsp agave syrup or maple syrup
- 1 clove garlic (minced)
- 1/2 tsp grated ginger

Zucchini Fritters
with Plant Yogurt Dip

SERVES: 4   PREP TIME: 15 MIN   COOK TIME: 15 MIN

Instructions

1. Place the grated zucchinis in a clean kitchen towel and squeeze out excess moisture.
2. In a large bowl, combine the grated zucchinis, chickpea flour, nutritional yeast, minced garlic, baking powder, salt, and pepper. Mix well to form a thick batter.
3. Heat a non-stick skillet over medium heat and add a thin layer of olive oil.
4. Drop spoonfuls of the zucchini batter onto the skillet, gently flattening them with the back of the spoon to form fritters.
5. Cook the fritters for 3-4 minutes on each side, or until they are golden brown and crispy.
6. Place the cooked fritters on a plate lined with paper towels to absorb any excess oil.
7. Serve the zucchini fritters warm with a side of vegan yogurt or a dipping sauce of your choice.

Ingredients

- 2 medium zucchinis (grated)
- 1/4 cup chickpea flour
- 1/4 cup nutritional yeast
- 2 cloves garlic (minced)
- 1/4 tsp baking powder
- Salt and pepper to taste
- Olive oil (for frying)

Tips:
- Feel free to add finely chopped onions or scallions to the batter for extra flavor.
- Make a lemon-dill sauce by mixing together lemon juice, vegan mayo, and chopped dill to drizzle over the fritters.

Watermelon, Feta, and Mint Salad

SERVES: 4　　　　　PREP TIME: 15 MIN　　　　　COOK TIME: 0 MIN

Instructions

1. In a large serving bowl, combine the cubed watermelon and crumbled vegan feta cheese.
2. Sprinkle the chopped fresh mint leaves over the watermelon and feta mixture.
3. Drizzle the balsamic glaze over the salad for a delightful tangy-sweet contrast.
4. Gently toss the salad to combine all the ingredients.
5. Serve this refreshing watermelon, feta, and mint salad as a light and delicious side dish.

Tips:

- If you can't find vegan feta cheese, you can substitute it with other vegan cheese cubes
- To make your own balsamic glaze, simmer balsamic vinegar in a small saucepan over low heat until it thickens and becomes syrupy.

Ingredients

- 4 cups cubed watermelon
- 1/2 cup vegan feta cheese (store-bought or homemade)
- Fresh mint leaves (chopped)
- Balsamic glaze (store-bought or homemade)

Greek Souvlaki with Tzatziki

SERVES: 4　　　　PREP TIME: 10 MIN　　　　BAKE TIME: 15 MIN

Instructions

Souvlaki

1. In a shallow dish, combine the olive oil, lemon juice, red wine vinegar, minced garlic, dried oregano, dried thyme, dried rosemary, dried basil, salt, and pepper to make the marinade.
2. Add the tofu or seitan cubes to the marinade, making sure they are well coated. Cover the dish or seal the bag, then refrigerate for at least 1-2 hours (or preferably overnight) to marinate.
3. When ready to cook, preheat a grill or grill pan over medium-high heat.
4. Thread the marinated tofu cubes onto skewers, if desired, for easy grilling..
5. Grill the tofu skewers for about 4-5 minutes on each side, or until they become crispy.

Tzatziki

1. In a bowl, mix together the ingredients for the Tzatziki. Adjust the seasoning to taste.
2. Cover and refrigerate the tzatziki sauce for at least 30 minutes to allow the flavors to meld.

Tips:

- make sure to press the Tofi before marinating to remove excess water and improve the texture.
- Customize the toppings to your liking by adding olives, roasted red peppers, or pickled onions.
- You can also serve the souvlaki with a side salad or roasted veggies and fries.

Ingredients

Souvlaki

- 400g firm tofu, cut into cubes
- 1/4 cup olive oil
- 3 tbsp lemon juice
- 2 tbsp red wine vinegar
- 2 cloves garlic, minced
- 1 tsp dried oregano
- 1 tsp dried thyme
- 1/2 tsp dried rosemary
- 1/2 tsp dried basil
- Salt and pepper to taste

Tzatziki

- 1 cup dairy-free plain yogurt (coconut or almond-based)
- 1/2 cucumber, grated and squeezed to remove excess water
- 2 cloves garlic, minced
- 1 tbsp lemon juice
- 1 tbsp fresh dill, chopped
- Salt and pepper to taste

Grilled Vegetable Skewers

SERVES: 4   PREP TIME: 20 MIN   COOK TIME: 10 MIN

Instructions

1. If using wooden skewers, soak them in water for at least 30 minutes before grilling to prevent burning.
2. In a large mixing bowl, combine the sliced zucchini, red and yellow bell pepper chunks, red onion chunks, and cherry tomatoes.
3. In a small bowl, whisk together the olive oil, minced garlic, balsamic vinegar, dried oregano, salt, and pepper to create the marinade.
4. Pour the marinade over the vegetables and toss until they are evenly coated.
5. Thread the marinated vegetables onto the skewers, alternating between different colors and types of vegetables.
6. Preheat your grill to medium-high heat. Grill the vegetable skewers for about 8-10 minutes, turning occasionally, until they are slightly charred and cooked to your desired tenderness.
7. Remove the skewers from the grill and serve them as a tasty and colorful side dish.

Tips:
- Add a sprinkle of lemon juice or a drizzle of balsamic glaze over the grilled vegetable skewers for extra flavor.
- You can also use other vegetables like mushrooms, eggplant, or asparagus in the skewers.
- Fot a little more protein, add cubed tofu.

Ingredients

- 1 zucchini (sliced into rounds)
- 1 red bell pepper (cut into chunks)
- 1 yellow bell pepper (cut into chunks)
- 1 red onion (cut into chunks)
- Cherry tomatoes
- 2 tbsps olive oil
- 2 cloves garlic (minced)
- 1 tbsp balsamic vinegar
- 1 tsp dried oregano
- Salt and pepper to taste
- Metal or wooden skewers

Vegan Sushi Rolls

SERVES: 1   PREP TIME: 30 MIN   COOK TIME: 0 MIN

Instructions

1. Place a bamboo sushi rolling mat on a clean surface and cover it with plastic wrap.
2. Lay one nori seaweed sheet on top of the rolling mat, shiny side down.
3. Wet your fingers with water to prevent the rice from sticking, then spread a thin layer of sushi rice over the nori, leaving a small border at the top edge.
4. Arrange the sliced vegetables and pickled ginger horizontally on the rice, near the bottom edge of the nori.
5. Carefully lift the bottom edge of the nori and the rolling mat, and start rolling the sushi away from you, using gentle pressure to shape it into a tight cylinder.
6. Continue rolling until you reach the top edge of the nori, moisten the border with water, and press to seal the roll.
7. Repeat the process to make additional sushi rolls.
8. Use a sharp knife to slice each roll into bite-sized pieces.
9. Serve the vegan sushi rolls with pickled ginger, wasabi, and soy sauce or tamari for dipping.

Ingredients

- 4 nori seaweed sheets
- 1 cup cooked sushi rice (seasoned with rice vinegar, sugar, and salt)
- Assorted sliced vegetables (e.g., cucumber, avocado, carrot, bell pepper)
- Pickled ginger
- Wasabi
- Soy sauce or tamari for dipping

Tips:
- Get creative with the fillings by adding marinated tofu, sautéed mushrooms, or vegan cream cheese.
- Use a sharp, wet knife when slicing the rolls to achieve clean cuts.

Lentil Shepherd's Pie

SERVES: 2 - 3   PREP TIME: 20 MIN   COOK TIME: 35 MIN

Instructions

1. Preheat the oven to 375°F (190°C).
2. In a large skillet, heat the olive oil over medium heat. Add the chopped onion, diced carrots, and diced celery. Sauté until the vegetables are softened.
3. Stir in the minced garlic and cook for an additional minute.
4. Add the cooked green lentils, frozen peas, tomato paste, soy sauce (or tamari), balsamic vinegar, dried thyme, dried rosemary, and smoked paprika. Mix everything together and cook for a few minutes until heated through. Season with salt and pepper to taste.
5. Transfer the lentil and vegetable mixture to a baking dish and spread it out evenly.
6. Top the lentil mixture with a layer of mashed potatoes, spreading them out evenly over the filling.
7. Use a fork to create a pattern on the mashed potatoes, which will help them brown in the oven.
8. Bake the vegan lentil shepherd's pie in the preheated oven for about 20 minutes or until the mashed potatoes are golden and slightly crispy on top.
9. Allow the shepherd's pie to cool slightly before serving.

Ingredients

- 1 cup green lentils (cooked)
- 1 tbsp olive oil
- 1 onion (finely chopped)
- 2 carrots (diced)
- 2 celery stalks (diced)
- 1 cup frozen peas
- 2 cloves garlic (minced)
- 1 tbsp tomato paste
- 1 tbsp soy sauce or tamari
- 1 tbsp balsamic vinegar
- 1 tsp dried thyme
- 1 tsp dried rosemary
- 1/2 tsp smoked paprika
- 4 cups mashed potatoes (prepared)
- Salt and pepper to taste

Tips:
- You can make the mashed potatoes using your preferred method, such as boiling and mashing potatoes with plant-based milk and vegan butter.
- Feel free to add other vegetables like corn or green beans to the lentil filling.

Summary Pasta Salad

SERVES: 4 - 6   PREP TIME: 15 MIN   COOK TIME: 15 MIN

Instructions

1. Cook the gluten-free pasta according to the package instructions until al dente. Drain and rinse the pasta under cold water to stop the cooking process. Let it cool to room temperature.
2. In a large mixing bowl, combine the cooked and cooled pasta, halved cherry tomatoes, diced cucumber, diced red bell pepper, diced yellow bell pepper, onion, sliced black olives, chopped fresh basil, chopped fresh parsley, and capers (if using).
3. In a separate small bowl, whisk together the extra-virgin olive oil, balsamic vinegar, Dijon mustard, minced garlic, salt, and pepper to create the dressing.
4. Pour the dressing over the pasta and vegetable mixture and toss everything together until well coated.
5. Chill the vegan gluten-free summer pasta salad in the refrigerator for at least 30 minutes before serving to allow the flavors to set.

Tips:
- Feel free to add other summer vegetables such as diced zucchini, corn kernels, or artichoke hearts for additional flavor and texture.
- If you prefer a creamier pasta salad, you can add a few tbsps of dairy-free mayonnaise or vegan sour cream to the dressing.
- This salad keeps well in the refrigerator for a few days, making it perfect for meal prep or leftovers.

Ingredients

- 8 oz gluten-free pasta (such as rice, corn, or quinoa pasta)
- 1 cup cherry tomatoes, halved
- 1 cup diced cucumber
- 1/2 cup diced red bell pepper
- 1/2 cup diced yellow bell pepper
- 1/4 cup sliced black olives
- 1/4 cup chopped fresh basil and parsley
- 1/2 red onion, chopped
- 2 tbsps capers (optional, for extra tang)
- 1/4 cup extra-virgin olive oil
- 2 tbsps balsamic vinegar
- 1 tbsp Dijon mustard
- 1 clove garlic, minced
- Salt and pepper to taste

Greek Salad

Instructions

1. In a large salad bowl, combine the diced cucumber, halved cherry tomatoes, thinly sliced red onion, sliced black olives, and crumbled vegan feta cheese.
2. In a small bowl, whisk together the fresh lemon juice, extra-virgin olive oil, dried oregano, salt, and pepper to make the dressing.
3. Drizzle the dressing over the salad and toss gently to combine all the ingredients.
4. Serve the refreshing and flavorful vegan Greek salad as a light and satisfying side dish or main course.

Tips:
- If you prefer a creamier dressing, you can add a spoonful of hummus or tahini to the lemon-olive oil mixture. (this is not traditional)
- Sprinkle some chopped fresh dill on top for an extra burst of Greek flavor.
- Greek salad is traditionally made without lettuce. If you prefer, you can add a cup of chopped .lettuce.

Ingredients

- 1 cucumber (diced)
- 1 cup cherry tomatoes (halved)
- 1/2 red onion (thinly sliced)
- 1/2 cup sliced black olives
- 1/4 cup vegan feta cheese (store-bought or homemade)
- 2 tbsps fresh lemon juice
- 2 tbsps extra-virgin olive oil
- 1 tsp dried oregano
- Salt and pepper to taste

Corn Chowder

SERVES: 2   PREP TIME: 10 MIN   COOK TIME: 25 MIN

Instructions

1. In a large pot, heat the olive oil over medium heat. Add the diced onion and minced garlic, and sauté until the onion becomes translucent.
2. Stir in the corn kernels and diced potatoes, and cook for a few minutes to slightly soften the vegetables.
3. Pour in the vegetable broth and bring the mixture to a boil. Reduce the heat to low, cover the pot, and simmer for about 15-20 minutes or until the potatoes are tender.
4. Add the unsweetened almond milk, dried thyme, and smoked paprika to the pot. Stir well and let the soup simmer for another 5 minutes.
5. Season the corn chowder with salt and pepper to taste.
6. Ladle the hot vegan corn chowder into serving bowls and garnish with chopped fresh chives before serving.

Ingredients

- 1 tbsp olive oil
- 1 onion (diced)
- 2 cloves garlic (minced)
- 2 cups fresh or frozen corn kernels
- 2 large potatoes (peeled and diced)
- 4 cups vegetable broth
- 1 cup unsweetened almond milk (or other plant-based milk)
- 1 tsp dried thyme
- 1/2 tsp smoked paprika
- Salt and pepper to taste
- optional: Fresh chives (chopped, for garnish)

Tips:

- For a creamier chowder, you can blend a portion of the soup before adding the almond milk.
- Sprinkle some vegan bacon bits or coconut bacon on top for added flavor and texture.

Summer Vegetable Curry

SERVES: 4　　　　PREP TIME: 15 MIN　　　　COOK TIME: 25 MIN

Instructions

1. In a large pot or skillet, heat the oil over medium heat. Add the onion and sauté until it becomes translucent.
2. Stir in the minced garlic and grated ginger. Cook for another minute until fragrant.
3. Add the diced red bell pepper, zucchini, and halved cherry tomatoes to the pot. Sauté for a few minutes until the vegetables start to soften.
4. Add the drained and rinsed chickpeas and pour in the coconut milk. Stir everything together.
5. Sprinkle the curry powder, ground cumin, ground coriander, turmeric, paprika, salt, and pepper over the mixture. Stir to coat the vegetables and chickpeas with the spices.
6. Cover the pot and let the curry simmer over medium-low heat for about 15-20 minutes, allowing the flavors to meld and the vegetables to become tender.
7. Taste the curry and adjust the seasoning if needed.
8. Serve the seasonal vegan gluten-free summer vegetable curry over cooked jasmine rice or with gluten-free naan. Garnish with fresh basil or cilantro if desired.

Tips:
- Feel free to incorporate other seasonal vegetables like corn, eggplant, or summer squash for added variety.
- For a touch of sweetness, you can add a handful of fresh diced peaches or mangoes to the curry during the last few minutes of cooking.

Ingredients

- 1 tbsp coconut oil
- 1 onion, chopped
- 3 cloves garlic, minced
- 1-inch piece of fresh ginger, grated
- 1 red bell pepper, diced
- 2 zucchinis, diced
- 1 cup cherry tomatoes, halved
- 1 can (15 oz) chickpeas, drained and rinsed
- 1 can (14 oz) coconut milk
- 2 tbsps curry powder
- 1 tsp ground cumin
- 1/2 tsp ground coriander
- 1/2 tsp turmeric
- 1/2 tsp paprika
- Salt and pepper to taste
- Fresh basil or cilantro for garnish (optional)
- Cooked jasmine rice for serving

Ratatouille

SERVES: 4   PREP TIME: 20 MIN   COOK TIME: 30 MIN

Instructions

1. In a large skillet or pot, heat the olive oil over medium heat. Add the sliced onion and minced garlic, and sauté until the onion becomes translucent.
2. Add the eggplant chunks to the skillet and cook for a few minutes until they start to soften.
3. Stir in the zucchini, yellow bell pepper, and red bell pepper, and continue to sauté the vegetables until they are tender-crisp.
4. Pour in the diced tomatoes and tomato paste, and stir well to combine.
5. Add the dried thyme and dried oregano to the skillet, and season with salt and pepper to taste.
6. Let the ratatouille simmer over medium-low heat for about 15-20 minutes to allow the flavors to meld.
7. Garnish the vegan ratatouille with chopped fresh basil leaves before serving.

Tips:
- For added richness, you can drizzle some extra-virgin olive oil over the ratatouille before serving.
- Serve the ratatouille with crusty bread or cooked quinoa for a complete meal.

Ingredients

- 2 tbsps olive oil
- 1 onion (sliced)
- 2 cloves garlic (minced)
- 1 eggplant (cut into chunks)
- 1 zucchini (cut into chunks)
- 1 yellow bell pepper (cut into chunks)
- 1 red bell pepper (cut into chunks)
- 1 can (14 oz) diced tomatoes
- 2 tbsps tomato paste
- 1 tsp dried thyme
- 1 tsp dried oregano
- Salt and pepper to taste
- Fresh basil leaves (chopped, for garnish)

Jackfruit Tacos

SERVES: 4   PREP TIME: 20 MIN   COOK TIME: 30 MIN

Instructions

1. Drain and rinse the young green jackfruit, and then use your hands to shred it into smaller pieces that resemble pulled pork or chicken.
2. In a large skillet, heat the olive oil over medium heat. Add the diced onion and minced garlic, and sauté until the onion becomes translucent.
3. Add the shredded jackfruit to the skillet, and stir in the chili powder, cumin, smoked paprika, salt, and pepper. Mix well to coat the jackfruit with the spices.
4. Pour the vegetable broth into the skillet, and bring the mixture to a simmer. Let it cook for about 10-15 minutes, or until the jackfruit becomes tender and absorbs the flavors.
5. While the jackfruit is cooking, warm the corn tortillas by heating them in a dry skillet for a few seconds on each side or microwaving them with a damp paper towel for a few seconds.
6. Assemble the tacos.
7. Serve the vegan jackfruit tacos with your favorite toppings such as shredded lettuce, diced tomatoes, avocado slices, cilantro, and a squeeze of lime juice.

Tips:
- You can also add a splash of lime juice and a pinch of cayenne pepper for an extra burst of flavor.
- Customize the tacos by adding vegan sour cream, salsa, or guacamole for extra creaminess and tanginess.

Ingredients

- 1 can (20 oz) young green jackfruit in brine (drained and rinsed)
- 1 tbsp olive oil
- 1/2 onion (diced)
- 2 cloves garlic (minced)
- 1 tbsp chili powder
- 1 tsp cumin
- 1/2 tsp smoked paprika
- Salt and pepper to taste
- 1/2 cup vegetable broth
- 8 small corn tortillas

Sweet Potato and Black Bean Burritos

SERVES: 4   PREP TIME: 20 MIN   COOK TIME: 25 MIN

Instructions

1. Preheat the oven to 400°F (200°C).
2. On a baking sheet, toss the diced sweet potatoes with olive oil, ground cumin, chili powder, salt, and pepper.
3. Roast the sweet potatoes in the preheated oven for about 20-25 minutes or until they are tender and slightly caramelized.
4. In a small saucepan, heat the black beans over medium heat. Season with salt and pepper, and cook until the beans are heated through.
5. Warm the flour tortillas in a dry skillet for a few seconds on each side.
6. Assemble the burritos by placing a portion of the roasted sweet potatoes and black beans in the center of each tortilla.
7. Add sliced avocado, salsa, and fresh cilantro on top of the filling.
8. Fold the sides of the tortilla inward, and then roll it up tightly to form the burrito.
9. Serve the flavorful and hearty vegan sweet potato and black bean burritos as a satisfying meal.

Ingredients

- 2 large sweet potatoes, peeled and diced
- 1 tbsp olive oil
- 1 can (15 oz) black beans, drained and rinsed
- 1 tsp ground cumin
- 1 tsp chili powder
- Salt and pepper to taste
- 4 large gluten free tortillas
- Sliced avocado, salsa, and fresh cilantro (for serving)

Tips:
- For extra creaminess, add a dollop of vegan sour cream or cashew cheese inside the burritos.
- Customize the burritos with your favorite vegetables or hot sauce.

Lemon Herb Roasted Baby Potatoes

SERVES: 4   PREP TIME: 10 MIN   COOK TIME: 25 MIN

Instructions

1. Preheat your oven to 425°F (220°C).
2. In a large mixing bowl, combine the halved baby potatoes, olive oil, fresh lemon juice, minced garlic, fresh thyme, fresh rosemary, paprika, salt, and pepper. Toss everything together until the potatoes are evenly coated with the seasoning.
3. Spread the seasoned baby potatoes in a single layer on a baking sheet lined with parchment paper or a silicone baking mat.
4. Roast the potatoes in the preheated oven for about 20-25 minutes or until they are tender and slightly crispy on the edges. Give them a gentle stir halfway through the roasting time to ensure even cooking.
5. Once the baby potatoes are done, remove them from the oven and transfer them to a serving dish.
6. Optionally, garnish with fresh parsley before serving for added freshness and color.

Tips:
- You can use a mix of different colored baby potatoes to make the dish visually appealing.
- Feel free to customize the herb seasoning to your liking, using your favorite herbs such as basil, oregano, or dill.
- These lemon herb roasted baby potatoes pair well with grilled vegetables, plant-based burgers, or your favorite vegan summer dishes. Enjoy!

Ingredients

- 1.5 lbs baby potatoes, washed and halved
- 2 tbsps olive oil
- 2 tbsps fresh lemon juice
- 2 cloves garlic, minced
- 1 tbsp fresh thyme leaves (or 1 tsp dried thyme)
- 1 tbsp fresh rosemary leaves (or 1 tsp dried rosemary)
- 1/2 tsp paprika
- Salt and pepper to taste
- Fresh parsley for garnish (optional)

Crispy Baked Zucchini Fries

SERVES: 2 - 4   PREP TIME: 15 MIN   COOK TIME: 20 - 25 MIN

Instructions

1. Preheat your oven to 425°F (220°C). Line a baking sheet with parchment paper.
2. In a shallow dish, combine the gluten-free bread crumbs, nutritional yeast, garlic powder, paprika, salt, and pepper. Mix well to create the coating mixture.
3. In a separate bowl, mix the unsweetened almond milk and olive oil.
4. Dip each zucchini strip into the almond milk mixture, coating it completely.
5. Then, roll the zucchini strip in the breadcrumb mixture, pressing down gently to ensure the coating sticks.
6. Place the coated zucchini strip on the prepared baking sheet. Repeat the process with the remaining zucchini.
7. Bake the zucchini fries in the preheated oven for about 20-25 minutes, or until they are golden and crispy, turning them over halfway through to ensure even browning.
8. Once baked, remove the zucchini fries from the oven and let them cool slightly before serving.
9. Serve the crispy baked zucchini fries with your favorite vegan dipping sauce for a flavorful and satisfying appetizer.

Ingredients

- 2 medium zucchinis, cut into fry-shaped strips
- 1/2 cup gluten-free bread crumbs
- 1/4 cup nutritional yeast
- 1 tsp garlic powder
- 1/2 tsp paprika
- Salt and pepper to taste
- 1/2 cup unsweetened almond milk (or any plant-based milk)
- 1 tbsp olive oil
- Vegan dipping sauce of your choice (e.g., marinara, vegan ranch, or garlic aioli)

Tips:
- For added flavor, you can mix in some dried herbs like oregano, basil, or thyme into the breadcrumb mixture.
- These zucchini fries are best served fresh and crispy, but you can reheat them in the oven for a few minutes at 350°F (175°C) if needed.

Thank You!

As we come to the end of this delicious journey together, I want to express my heartfelt appreciation to each and every one of you. Your presence and support have made our gluten-free vegan summer cookbook a truly heartwarming experience.

To all the wonderful recipe testers, food enthusiasts, and compassionate souls out there, your valuable feedback and endless encouragement have been the driving force behind this labor of love. Your passion for embracing a wholesome, gluten-free vegan lifestyle fills me with inspiration to keep exploring the wonderful world of plant-based cuisine.

A special thanks goes out to the dedicated farmers and growers who have lovingly nurtured the seasonal delights we've celebrated throughout these pages. Your commitment to sustainable practices is a reminder of the beautiful connection between food and nature.

To those who have welcomed this cookbook into their homes and hearts, I wish you countless joyful culinary adventures filled with creativity and the joy of sharing nourishing meals with your loved ones.

As we say goodbye for now, let's carry the spirit of compassion, mindfulness, and seasonal living into our daily lives. Together, let's continue to create a world where well-being and harmony thrive.

I'm looking forward to embarking on a new season with you all, discovering the warm and comforting flavors of autumn and embracing the abundance that nature has in store for us. Thank you, dear readers, for being an essential part of this beautiful journey. Until we meet again, may your summer days be abundant with flavor, love, and the simple joys of gluten-free vegan living.

With heartfelt gratitude,

Stella Blackwell

Please note that the availability of these foods may vary slightly depending on your geographical location and climate. Enjoy the diverse and delicious variety of seasonal produce during each month!

Sources:

- Bazzano, L. A., He, J., Ogden, L. G., Loria, C. M., Vupputuri, S., Myers, L., ... & Whelton, P. K. (2002). Fruit and vegetable intake and risk of cardiovascular disease in US adults: the first National Health and Nutrition Examination Survey Epidemiologic Follow-up Study. The American journal of clinical nutrition, 76(1), 93-99.
- Lavin, J. H., & Vinyard, B. T. (2013). Seasonal variation in the taste of tomatoes (Solanum lycopersicum) is lost under market-like conditions. PloS one, 8(11), e78605.
- FAO. (n.d.). Food and Agriculture Organization of the United Nations. Retrieved from http://www.fao.org/home/en/.
- Garnett, T. (2011). Where's the beef? The rise and fall of the Mediterranean cuisine and the industrialisation of the pig. Food & history, 8(2), 7-39.
- Ingram, J. (2001). Local food systems in old industrial regions: Apples and oranges?. The role of food, agriculture, forestry and fisheries in human nutrition, 303.
- Davis, D. R. (2009). Declining fruit and vegetable nutrient composition: what is the evidence?. HortScience, 44(1), 15-19.
- Kirchmann, H., & Thorvaldsson, G. (2000). Challenging targets for future agriculture. European Journal of Agronomy, 12(3-4), 145-161.
- Li, S., Zhang, J., Huang, J., & Xie, X. (2016). Effects of crop rotation on soil microbial community structure and function in continuously cropped land. Frontiers in Microbiology, 7, 161.
- Lal, R. (2015). Restoring soil quality to mitigate soil degradation. Sustainability, 7(5), 5875-5895.
- Drewnowski, A. (2019). The Nutrient-Rich Foods Index helps to identify healthy, affordable foods. The American Journal of Clinical Nutrition, 109(3), 457-458.
- Nestle, M. (1999). Modern Food, Moral Food: Self-Control, Science, and the Rise of Modern American Eating in the Early Twentieth Century. American Historical Review, 104(5), 1617-1618.